## Teens Talk About Being Gifted, Talented, or Otherwise Extra-Ordinary

# More Than a Test Score

**Teens Talk About Being Gifted,
Talented, or Otherwise Extra-Ordinary**

Robert A. Schultz, Ph.D.
James R. Delisle, Ph.D.

Illustrated by Tyler Page

free spirit
PUBLiSHiNG®

Helping kids
help themselves™
since 1983

**Library of Congress Cataloging-in-Publication Data**
Schultz, Robert A., 1962–
    More than a test score : teens talk about being gifted, talented, or otherwise extra-ordinary / Robert A. Schultz.
        p. cm.
    Includes index.
    ISBN-13: 978-1-57542-221-3
    ISBN-10: 1-57542-221-2
    1. Gifted teenagers. 2. Ability. 3. Expertise. I. Title.
    BF724.3.G53S38 2006
    155.5087'9—dc22

                                                                    2006025379

At the time of this book's publication, all facts and figures cited are the most current avail-able. All telephone numbers, addresses, and Web site URLs are accurate and active; all publications, organizations, Web sites, and other resources exist as described in this book; and all have been verified as of May 2006. The authors and Free Spirit Publishing make no warranty or guarantee concerning the information and materials given out by organiza-tions or content found at Web sites, and we are not responsible for any changes that occur after this book's publication. If you find an error or believe that a resource listed here is not as described, please contact Free Spirit Publishing. Parents, teachers, and other adults: We strongly urge you to monitor children's use of the Internet.

Edited by Eric Braun
Cover and interior design by Marti Naughton

10  9  8  7  6  5  4  3  2
Printed in the United States of America

**Free Spirit Publishing Inc.**
217 Fifth Avenue North, Suite 200
Minneapolis, MN 55401-1299
(612) 338-2068
help4kids@freespirit.com
www.freespirit.com

# Dedication

*To my young family (with the old parents): your lives inspire my work and engage my soul to make life better, each and every day. What journeys will we share in the coming years? All I know is we are along for the ride together. And that is all I need.*
—R.A.S.

*To my students at R.B. Chamberlin Middle School in Twinsburg, Ohio, countless thanks for the wisdom and joy you share with me so willingly every Wednesday. Collectively and individually, you are as much my teacher as I am yours.*
—J.R.D.

# Acknowledgments

Our unending gratitude to the thousands of gifted individuals around the world who contributed their time, energy, and emotions to this project. Special adulation is due to the "In Their Words" writers, who shared even more deeply of themselves. We hope we have done justice to the experiences, expectations, and information you all contributed. To Eric Braun, thank you for being a kind and thorough editor. Lastly, to our families and spouses, for their patience and support, our gratitude and love forever.

# Contents

# Introduction

I f you were to count the number of words that have been published about gifted children and teenagers, the final tally probably would be in the billions. That's because people have done a lot of research to try to understand giftedness better, and they've written about their findings.

Now, if you were to count the number of words published *by* gifted kids about what it means to be gifted, the number would be lower—way, way, lower.

That's why we created this book. We believe the people who best understand what it is like to grow up gifted are the individuals who wear the gifted label everyday: the 13-year-old who goes through school wondering when teachers will touch upon a topic that is new and meaningful to him; the 15-year-old who seeks a friend with whom she can use vocabulary that causes other classmates to say "huh?"; the 18-year-old who struggles to decide on a college major because so many of them sound interesting.

We wanted to give teenagers the voice that often is lacking in other publications about giftedness: *their own* voice. And that's what you'll find in *More Than a Test Score:* hundreds of gifted teens talking about the high points and hurdles they face every day.

Having grown up gifted ourselves, we know many of those high points and hurdles well. We know some people equate giftedness with social malfunction . . . and we know those people are wrong. We know some teachers look at gifted students and say, "You've got it easy, you're smart"—and use your intelligence as an excuse to ignore your learning needs—and we, too, resisted giving a response that would have landed us in perennial detention. We know that making a mistake often elicits a hurtful comment from an onlooker like, "I expected more from a kid with your abilities." Hey, more than anything else, you are a teenager first who just happens to be gifted, not a gifted person who happens to be a teen. It sounds like a small distinction, but it's not. When you live it every day, it's a very big difference. As a teenager, you deserve to be challenged in school and you have the right to make mistakes like every other human being.

## How This Book Came to Be

To find out what gifted teens had to say about giftedness, we asked them. We posted a questionnaire at our Web site, www.giftedkidspeak.com, starting in 2003, asking about school, friends, expectations, family life, the future, and anything else teens wanted to share. Thousands of individuals answered from the United States, Canada, and many other countries. In *More Than a Test Score,* we share some of the most common answers, as well as some of the most interesting and funny ones, from people ages 13 to 19.

We also gathered personal stories from gifted and/or talented teenagers we have come to know. These brief biographies, called "In Their Words," are sprinkled throughout the book and give you an even deeper look into the minds and lives of other gifted teens.

## Reading This Book: A User's Guide

This is your book (even if on loan from a friend or library), so we're not going to tell you how to read it. Start in the middle and skip around, if you like. Seek out responses to questions that are important to you right now (the "Contents" lists all the questions and where to find them), or read only the comments made by others your age (responses are listed from youngest to oldest). You can even start at the beginning and go straight through to the end! You can learn from and enjoy this book no matter how you approach it.

As you read the questions and responses from gifted teens, think about how *you* would answer the questions. If you want, write down some answers. You'll also find "Reflection/Connection" boxes throughout that can help you explore more deeply the issues raised by the questions.

Finally, think about how the responses compare to your own thoughts and experiences. Which ones sound like something you would say (or have said)? Which ones don't sound right? And what can you learn from the difference between the two? Are there any ideas you never thought of before? If so, could those new ideas help you handle an issue you're wrestling with?

We hope you learn as much about giftedness (and yourself) from reading this book as we did in compiling it. We hope, too, that in reading about other gifted teens, you'll feel like a part of a community in a world where giftedness is still a rarity.

If you would like to contribute to this community with a comment of your own, we're only a few clicks away. Write to us at the address below or visit www.giftedkidspeak.com and post your answers to the survey questions. Or, for that matter, raise your own question and answer it; we'll listen. Either way, you'll be continuing the dialogue about growing up gifted.

Enjoy our book. Enjoy your life.

**Bob Schultz and Jim Delisle**
Free Spirit Publishing
217 Fifth Avenue North, Suite 200
Minneapolis, MN 55401-1299
help4kids@freespirit.com

# What Does It Mean to Be a Gifted Teen?

**T**here are as many ways to interpret giftedness as there are people to interpret it. "Giftedness" is more than a test score and more than a label—it affects all parts of your life (not just school!). It can be tricky figuring out what giftedness means to you since giftedness is so central to who you are. How can you strip away that part of yourself to see what's left?

In this chapter you won't find simple answers to the meaning of giftedness. Instead, you'll find something deeper and more complex: hundreds of diverse insights about the many benefits and problems that gifted teens encounter.

## What do you think being gifted means, and what is your reaction to this term?

Giftedness is having exceptional abilities and being motivated enough to use those abilities to create wonderful things.

Girl, 13, Iowa

"Gifted" is something that is used very lightly around me. I'm called "smart," "talented," and "bright," but it's very few times that someone refers to me as gifted. It's a touchy subject, really.

Girl, 13, Australia

When people ask if I am gifted, I am usually silent because I am ridiculed for being smart. It gets very difficult because I can't use my entire abilities on a subject.

Boy, 13, Iowa

Being gifted means having an ability to learn things faster. My reaction to the term is "I'm not gifted." I just work hard. I think calling exceptionally smart people "gifted" takes credit away from their hard work and effort and says "they were just born that way."

Girl, 13, Oklahoma

Giftedness means you can think on your feet, be creative, and express yourself.

Girl, 13, New Jersey

**"It's a touchy subject, really."**

The term "gifted" seems to be used more loosely than it used to be and I think it should be used more strictly.

Boy, 14, Ohio

Some people think that I'm supposed to be somewhat of a brainiac when I tell them that I'm gifted, but I'm really not. I just have an extended ability to take information in a lot faster.

Boy, 14, Texas

When I hear the word "gifted," I think that I am more likely to do the right things and follow the right path in life.
Boy, 14, Illinois

I think that being gifted means that I am maybe a little more dedicated and smarter than some others. My reaction toward the term gifted? I basically think of nerds, which means I think I am a nerd, but also, at the same time, I don't feel like one.
Girl, 14, Texas

There are regular Joe Blows who could be gifted if they would just focus.
Boy, 14, Ohio

Personally, I don't think that being picked out as gifted is anything special. I'm just your Average Joe. I think being gifted is just a fable that teachers use to give us harder work.
Boy, 14, Nebraska

Being gifted is a state of mind. It is liking adult (not rude, but more mature) humor, debating issues, being interested in the world, and wanting to make a difference. It's wanting to be perfect.
Girl, 14, England

I think the term "gifted" is appropriate, but it's not one I'd pick, because it gets people defensive.
Boy, 14, Massachusetts

Gifted means that you look at the world from a totally different perspective.
Girl, 15, New Mexico

What gifted means to me is that my brain works so much faster than most people around me that it is hard to maintain interest in conversations. (Why is it so hard to state this fact without sounding like I'm bragging or lying?)
Boy, 15, North Carolina

Being gifted means that you absorb stuff around you—you catch on to concepts quicker than those around you.

Girl, 15, Tennessee

My reaction to the term gifted depends on the circumstances. If it is one of my friends calling me gifted, I feel embarrassment. If it is an adult saying the term gifted, I do not feel any sudden emotion.

Boy, 15, New York

Being gifted means getting to miss class and do fun stuff in elementary school and being bored in class in later years. It means nothing other than adults need a euphemism for "smart" because they just can't say I'm "smart" and put me in the "smart classes" that my parents were in in the '60s and '70s.

Girl, 15, Wisconsin

Gifted means you can forget to study and still do well on "the big test."

Girl, 16, Texas

My reaction to the word gifted is always the same: "Are you talking to *me*?"

Boy, 16, Ohio

"You look at the world from a totally different perspective."

Gifted can't really be defined, in my opinion. It means something slightly different to everyone, with gifted people being even more diverse in their definitions than anyone else.

Boy, 16, Iowa

I'm not sure if I agree with using the term "gifted," because aren't other children blessed with "gifts" that are not necessarily a smart mind?

Girl, 16, Florida

I do not like the term gifted. I believe it puts young people on a platform that is not always earned.

Boy, 17, Tennessee

People who are gifted have abilities that are not commonplace, such as the ability to multiply triple or quadruple digit numbers in their head. Gifted is not so much a type of person as it is a state of mind that has developed beyond its age.

Boy, 17, Kentucky

Being gifted, I can form connections in ways that your average student can't. When I learn something in history class that relates to something in English class, I have a much better chance of putting two and two together.

Boy, 18, Virginia

I always hated the term "gifted." I mean, I was always more or less set apart from the other kids in school, and being labeled gifted just made it worse. It gave them one more thing to tease me about.

Girl, 19, North Carolina

# Reflection Connection

Many gifted teens have a negative view of the term "gifted," for various reasons. Some think it's elitist, others find it too vague, and yet others see it as just (as one student responded) "a fable that teachers use to give us harder work." How do you feel about the term "gifted"? If you don't like it, what would you suggest as a replacement?

## How did you find out that you are gifted?

What kind of question is this? It's not like I'm a mutation or something. It's not like "one day I looked at a test and IT WAS REALLY EASY! AIEE." Gifted is just something you are.

Boy, 13, Massachusetts

My mom just told me I was gifted. In my family, we're all gifted.

Boy, 13, Maine

I always knew. I was always different from the other kids.

Girl, 13, New Jersey

I had always been raised with the idea, and then I came across a book with gifted characters and saw how much I could relate.

Girl, 13, Massachusetts

I realized it through music, when I was good at the violin and trombone even if I didn't practice. But also, I seemed to have a better memory than others and understood things more quickly.

Boy, 13, New Jersey

I knew I was smart even before my teachers reminded me that I was. My grandmother told me I was gifted even before I ever went to school. Now, isn't that amazing? I was like 4 or 5 years old.

Girl, 13, Louisiana

I'll admit it: I wasn't smart at all. It wasn't until my teacher took time after school to help me. In doing so, she unlocked my gift and I started excelling at everything.

Girl, 14, Texas

I realized I was gifted in kindergarten when none of the other kids wanted to read *Babysitter Club* books with me.

Girl, 14, Massachusetts

I've always known that I've been gifted. Still, it's kind of weird knowing that you are smarter than most of your friends.

Boy, 14, Illinois

I never "found out." People just told me I was smart. They bussed me far away to be with other "smart kids." They kept telling us we were gifted, different, set apart. So I learned to be that way.

Girl, 14, Minnesota

I found out when one of my earlier teachers signed me up to take a special test and I passed, proving I was gifted.

Boy, 14, Texas

When I was younger, I used to blurt out answers all the time. One of my teachers suspected that I might be gifted. I was then examined and approved to be in the gifted program.

Girl, 14, Oklahoma

Research. I simply saw what I was doing, what others were doing, did a bit of digging around, a lot of questioning, and came to the conclusion that I probably qualified as gifted. I mean, they were reading *Clifford;* I was reading *Hamlet.*

Girl, 14, Australia

> "I mean, they were reading CLIFFORD; I was reading HAMLET."

I found out I was gifted in first grade. Every assignment that was given to me I would complete before the teacher would say "start."

Boy, 14, Texas

When I met other family members, their first comment would be, "So, this is the genius?"

Boy, 15, Utah

In school, I was always so bored. I had a system: pay attention on Monday, then daydream and doodle until Friday, when I would pass whatever tests they gave me, because it was reviewed the whole week. I hated it. So my mother had me tested and they figured I was gifted, and I went to a different school.

Girl, 15, Connecticut

I was evaluated in eighth grade because my teachers said that I looked bored with my work.

Boy, 16, Minnesota

I asked my third-grade teacher to nominate me for the gifted program because we both knew I was smarter than the rest of my classmates. She did, and I was.

Boy, 16, California

I didn't really understand what giftedness was until seventh grade, at which point my giftedness combined with my "cavalier attitude" to create the biggest clash I've ever had with . . . well, anything.

Boy, 16, Iowa

I think I knew I was gifted in fifth grade, when I had to have math when my grade had lunch, and I had to have lunch when they had math.

Girl, 16, Pennsylvania

One day, the gifted fairy came to my bedside and whispered in my ear the magic words to become gifted. The next day when I woke up, I had an intense headache, which would later be identified as my brain growing to an enormous size. (In other words, I was noticed in seventh grade, for my creativity.)

Boy, 16, Tennessee

When I was released into "regular" public school from my special ed classes in my inner-city neighborhood school, I noticed that many of the kids considered me "smart" and a "nerd," despite my goth/slacker image.

Girl, 17, New York

When I was in elementary school, I was in a Spanish immersion program. One of the classes taught in Spanish was math. When it became clear that not only did I have a better grasp on math than my teacher, but that I spoke better Spanish than she did, despite it being her first language and my second, there wasn't much doubt in anyone's mind.

Boy, 17, Virginia

When I was in first grade, my teacher had a discussion with my parents who later had a talk with me. When testing (which was fun and easy) determined I was gifted, my parents were very proud. Later, my mom said to me, "It's funny. Last year they wouldn't put you in kindergarten because you couldn't draw a perfect circle. Now they tell me your IQ results show you're gifted." Go figure.

Girl, 19, Pennsylvania

## Are there times when you try to hide that you are gifted?

I hide it because in fourth grade my friends found out and they ditched me. That is the worst feeling a kid can have.

Boy, 13, Ohio

In gifted classes, where everyone knows that you're gifted, no one really cares or thinks about it. Also, I have a crush on some of the guys in that class, so when I'm in it, I try to stick out with the fact that I'm gifted.

Girl, 13, Texas

At summer camp, I tried. I wanted to see what it was like to be normal. But it obviously didn't work, since all the counselors thought I was one of them.

Girl, 13, Ontario

I don't try to hide that I'm gifted, but I don't like the gifted label. Why can't they just say we are "normal with an edge"?

Boy, 13, Ohio

I especially try to fit in around other girls. I couldn't really care less if they think I'm a weirdo, but when a girl gets the idea that you would make a good "teasing target," it's worse than boys shouting insults at you. After all, the boys never mean it.

Girl, 13, Texas

Yes, I try to hide it because it gets annoying winning stuff and being gone for my gifted program. I won the spelling bee and am going to the state finals for Math Counts and people say stuff like, "Oh, there goes the champ."

Girl, 14, Wisconsin

> "I was always afraid that they would find out that I really liked to read and learn."

Yes, all the time, to fit in. I don't even do extra credit work anymore and I don't ask if I can work ahead.

Boy, 14, Iowa

I never try to hide the fact that I'm gifted. It is something that I am very proud of. I believe that if someone doesn't like it, they do not have to be my friend.

Girl, 14, Ohio

Sometimes I just want to be . . . relatively normal. But it doesn't work. I have to be me.

Boy, 14, Ohio

I do try to hide it because everyone wants the answers to everything and tries to cheat off me. When I say no, they get all mad.

Boy, 14, New York

Sometimes, when I'm just trying to fit in and have fun, I don't want to show people my differences. I don't push the fact that I'm gifted in the other people's faces. That would just turn them off. I usually appear the same as them and wait for them to discover on their own that I might have a gift.

Girl, 14, Maine

No. I think being gifted is part of who I am, and if you can't accept that, then I don't want to be around you.

Boy, 15, Ohio

No, because it's almost impossible to hide it. Besides, I like to brag.

Girl, 15, Wisconsin

No, I can't hide who I am. It's something I used to do, and it caused me immense stress. I was always afraid that they would find out that I really liked to read and learn. Since then, I've learned otherwise and am proud of who and what I am.

Boy, 15, Kansas

Usually, when I'm introduced to a new person, I "lower my intellect" so I don't scare them away. If they come back to talk to me, then I up the intellect.

Girl, 15, Tennessee

It just depends whether I'm around a mature group of people.

Girl, 16, Minnesota

I don't try to hide how smart I am, but I try not to say anything too weird, because then no one will know what I'm talking about, which is annoying because then you get these awkward pauses.

Boy, 16, Washington, DC

Yes, I sometimes hide it. I'm lazy, so if I underachieve, teachers expect less of me and I have a lot more time to do whatever I want, whether that be sports, drawing, or learning about autoimmune diseases.

Girl, 16, Indiana

Yes, there have been several times when I won't tell people about my gifted school or me being classified as gifted. The reason is when other kids hear my school's name, the first thing they say is, "He thinks he's better than us" and "He thinks he's all that." Actually, it's just the opposite: I just want to be a kid and just be me.

Boy, 16, Ohio

I just try to keep my mouth shut. It only makes others dislike me when I speak.

Girl, 17, South Carolina

Maybe I tried to hide it in middle school. But doesn't everyone try to hide who they are in middle school?

Girl, 18, Virginia

I have, unfortunately, lowered my standards so I do not fall from lofty heights in the eyes of my friends.

Boy, 18, Tennessee

I avoid telling strangers or casual acquaintances that I go to Yale, since it usually leads to an awkwardly congratulatory conversation about how smart I must be.

Girl, 19, Connecticut

"Doesn't everyone try to hide who they are in middle school?"

It would be hard for me to hide that I'm gifted, because the way I talk and think just screams "gifted!"

Girl, 19, North Carolina

## Reflection Connection

Some people have no trouble talking about or showing their giftedness to friends, but others seem more comfortable keeping their gifts hidden. What about you? Do you like others to know you're gifted, or do you prefer to keep it to yourself? Are there certain times when you feel more comfortable showing your giftedness? Are there times when it's harder? Why do you think that is?

## What are the best and worst parts about being gifted?

Best? I get to hold intelligent conversations with intelligent people. Also, I have enough intelligence to control my life and where I want to go with it. Worst? Discrimination: my abilities are held against me.

Girl, 13, Australia

The best things are being able to take advantage of better opportunities that are offered to me and being around other gifted people. The worst thing is the expectation that you should never make a mistake.

Boy, 14, Ohio

The best part is the recognition. The worst is the brand on my forehead. What? You can't see it? It seems everyone else can. I feel like a leper sometimes with so few people I can turn to. That necessary solitude must be the worst thing.

Girl, 14, Texas

The best part is that you know you have an above-average ability to make positive changes in society by using your talents. The worst thing is not really having a choice in the matter, and not knowing whether you can take credit for something that seems mainly enabled by accident of birth.

Girl, 14, Massachusetts

The best thing is how much you can learn. The worst thing is that you aren't learning it.

Boy, 14, Massachusetts

The best is my mom lets me do things kids my age don't usually do, like taking some practice SATs (it was boring and hard, but fun at the same time). The worst thing that has happened is that a friend got mad at me for reading books during lunch instead of talking to her. I thought this was stupid, because she never talked to me too much anyway. (She didn't like it when I pointed this out to her.)

Girl, 14, Texas

The best thing is I can enjoy certain things meant for older and more educated people. The worst is, people treat me like I'm better and different.

Boy, 15, California

Usually, my brain is my favorite playmate, but occasionally it turns traitor on me just when I need it the most. I hate that. I really can't address this question any better than this, because since I've always been gifted, I have no basis for comparison. Do I ask other people what it's like to be average?

Boy, 15, North Carolina

The best thing is all the doors it opens and all the recognition you get. The worst is also all the possibilities, because I have trouble choosing what I want to do—and people expect me to know.

Girl, 15, Iowa

The best part is that I feel free to speak my mind, but that could be my personality rather than my being gifted. The worst part is getting treated differently by everyone else who is not gifted.

Boy, 16, Illinois

The best thing about being called gifted? It looks good on college applications, I guess.

Boy, 16, Tennessee

Best: the teachers love us because we're the "good" kids. Worst: people judge you before they even know you.

Girl, 16, Oklahoma

"A friend got mad at me for reading books during lunch instead of talking to her."

Best: a lot of things come easily to me.
Worst: the high expectations never go away.

Boy, 16, Wisconsin

The loneliness is the worst. I'm from a VERY small school in a rural area and there aren't many other gifted kids around. I struggle with issues like religion, morality, philosophy, and politics, and there simply isn't anyone I can talk to about them. It leads me to feel I am very, very, very alone in this world. The best thing is the level of complexity I can comprehend. I love hard concepts that make me reorganize my ways of thinking. Sometimes, when the ideas are coming fast and heavy, it feels like my brain is dancing.

Boy, 17, Kansas

# In Their Words: Kellen, Age 18

Basketball: my passion, my future. Since I was old enough to bounce a ball, I figured I would someday give Michael Jordan a run for his money. I pictured myself running down the court as a packed house of spectators cheered wildly at my performance.

Well . . . I was right about the cheering crowds, but it wasn't basketball that brought them to their feet, it was my voice. Here's how it all started.

I'm an 18-year-old college freshman, having lived my whole life in a suburb of Cleveland, Ohio. Before college, I lived with my mom and, until he moved out two years ago, my older brother, Keith. We live in a very diverse community where tolerance for differences is the norm. Also, I lived down the street from a university, so it seemed like my backyard was always a college campus.

My mom knew how much I loved basketball but, being a mom, she wanted me to expand my interests. So, when I was 4, she put me in a church choir. I sang there for a while, but it

→

wasn't until eighth grade, when I entered a talent show with a four-man rhythm-and-blues group, that I began with some friends, that my musical horizons opened up. In front of my classmates, I sang a solo—and they gave me a standing ovation! Since this occurred at about the same time my basketball coach told me I didn't have the skills or the size to be the next Michael Jordan, I refocused my energies toward singing. I've never looked back.

I auditioned for a troupe called the "Singing Angels," and its national director, Jim Boehm, called me the same night I sang for him to tell me I was accepted into his troupe. I thought it was a joke! I couldn't read music then (in fact, I still can't), but if someone else sang a note or played one on the piano, I could echo the note perfectly. At age 14, I joined my school's a cappella choir, trying again to read music—with no luck. I guess it's just like those math whizzes who know the answer to a complex math problem without going through all the steps. I just knew how to sing and how to reach the notes I needed to hit.

As high school continued, I stuck with voice lessons and learned how to prepare my voice (drink licorice tea) and what to avoid before a performance (dairy products). I entered several contests for solo-ists, almost always winning awards of distinction. Then, I hit the big time: London, England.

For a sophomore in high school who had never ventured far from home, it was almost like make believe to be singing in Windsor Castle and Bath Abbey for hundreds of people. Michael Jordan I wasn't, but they applauded as loudly as if I'd just scored the winning three-pointer from center court. Next stop, San Francisco, where more and more people came to hear me sing. There was even an impromptu "concert" my friends and I gave in Terminal E at O'Hare Airport in Chicago. Wherever we sang, crowds gathered and cheered.

In the midst of all this happiness, turmoil engulfed my life: my parents were getting a divorce. Since Keith had moved out, it was just my mom and me at home. I knew she was down, and I tried to help in any ways I could. For example, I talked to her any time she needed me to, and I stayed at the house more often than usual . . . just to be there in case she needed me. Also, since money was even tighter than usual, I paid a few household bills with money from the job I had after school and on weekends. They weren't big bills, but even paying the cable bill, the water bill, or occasionally buying groceries seemed to help. I also suppported her by promising that I would continue to strive for a goal that was important to both of us: having my name in the graduation booklet for having a GPA of at least 3.0—and yes, I eventually did it!

Still, it was a hard time for me. My salvations were these: singing, school, and friendships. As long as I kept myself occupied, I was okay, but as soon as I was alone with my thoughts, things got tough again. During those times, I often felt lonely and afraid. I had realized that I needed to accept a situation that was hard to accept—my parents splitting up. Maybe I should have talked to someone about my feelings, but all my life I had kept my feelings bottled up, so that's what I did. I didn't want anyone else to know that I was hurting, especially my mom.

Then, two things happened that forged in me a new, positive attitude. First, I started talking to my friends about my parents' divorce, and I learned how many of them had gone through the same thing. I realized how lucky I actually was, as I got to be with my dad for sixteen years, while some of my friends never knew their dads at all. I began to see the positive side of something so negative. Second, a friend of mine got cancer in tenth grade, and it reappeared in twelfth grade despite surgeries and all types of therapies. Yet she always had a smile on her face and, in her own quiet way, gave me a perspective on life that I hadn't had before. As I wrote in her yearbook, "You are my hero and your example has made me a better person."

After all my successes in singing, my most memorable moment was when I sang our national anthem at my high school graduation. I'd been in the choir for three years, and when I entered the concert hall where our graduation took place, I said to myself, "Kellen, this year, you won't be *listening* to the soloist—you *will be* the soloist." I was more nervous singing in front of those hundreds of friends and family members than I was when I sang at the Cleveland Cavaliers basketball game, but when I sang the final note, the audience cheered wildly. All that night, classmates who had never heard me sing before called me up to congratulate me—one even said he never felt as patriotic as he did when he heard me sing "The Star-Spangled Banner." That made me prouder than if I *had* sunk the winning basket in a playoff game.

So . . . what's next? A college major in musical performance and a few acting classes, all to prepare for what I hope will be a career on Broadway or as an R+B recording artist. Maybe both. Until then, I'll keep shooting hoops, knowing that having fun, maintaining a positive attitude, and sticking with friends and family in good times and bad are the keys to success.

## Sometimes gifted people talk about intensities or passions rather than interests. What's the difference?

Interests come and go. Passions stay and overwhelm you.
Girl, 13, New Jersey

I have passions and intensities for law enforcement and airplanes. Interests are small, but intensities are what you would consider doing with your life.
Boy, 13, Ohio

I think I do have a bit of an obsessive strain, but only enough to be useful. I love to read, sometimes ten books a week, and there are books that I read ten times in a week. This has helped me to develop a unique writing style and that, coupled with an overly active imagination, has helped me complete a novel.
Girl, 13, Pennsylvania

"For me, writing is like breathing. I can't live without it."

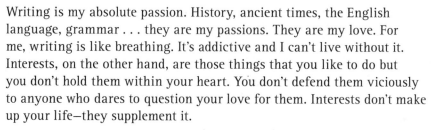 

Writing is my absolute passion. History, ancient times, the English language, grammar . . . they are my passions. They are my love. For me, writing is like breathing. It's addictive and I can't live without it. Interests, on the other hand, are those things that you like to do but you don't hold them within your heart. You don't defend them viciously to anyone who dares to question your love for them. Interests don't make up your life—they supplement it.

Girl, 14, Australia

I get obsessed about things more often than other people. I tend to stay interested in things or think famous guys are cute long after my peers think they are passé.

Girl, 14, England

The difference between passions and interests? Simple: semantics and access.

Boy, 15, Kentucky

Interests are pursued for entertainment. Passions are doggedly pursued for purpose, either the betterment of oneself or one's community. Honestly, I think my most profound passion is the search . . . for passion. Most frustrating of all is that among my peers, I sometimes feel alone in this quest.

Boy, 15, Wisconsin

Intensities and passions are things you can't live without. For me, that's music. It makes me happy and it makes me feel whole.

Girl, 15, Texas

Nothing important is accomplished by interest, it is accomplished by passion. It is the gifted person who makes life work for the average person.

Girl, 15, Indiana

The difference is that interests can be purely academic, while intensities or passions require a sense of personal involvement or care. The distinction is especially important in gifted individuals who are interested in just about everything.

Boy, 15, Maine

I am *definitely* a person with passions (obsessions, really). I have gone through *so many* obsessions: fairies, dinosaurs, cats, prehistoric humans, ants, and now, anime and manga. With a passion, you want to immerse yourself in it, learn everything about it, read all the books you can. You want to know what it's like to be a fairy, a dinosaur, a cat, a whatever. You want to live it.

Girl, 15, Illinois

The difference is what motivates you. For instance, I was interested to answer these questions through sheer force of curiosity (one of my strongest emotions), and it was fun. My opinions rarely matter, and I doubt that this will ever be read by many people, if anyone at all, but I wanted to answer them anyway. As far as a passion goes, I have no idea yet, since I've never had one, so the blind man isn't going to try calling the sun green.

Boy, 16, Iowa

Interests can come and go, like boyfriends and girlfriends, but passions last forever and they leave an imprint on you.

Girl, 16, Colorado

You get totally absorbed by your passions. You think about them at school, after school, when you're trying to sleep, and when you wake up in the morning. Your world is centered around them and you try to make whatever you can relate to them. I am currently passionless, and have been for a while. This makes me feel depressed and, to some extent, like my life lacks meaning.

Boy, 17, Kansas

A passion is something that I devote myself to, while an interest is more passive. I'm passionate about backpacking. I could backpack nonstop for a year and never get sick of it. (In fact, I intend to do this when I graduate college.) I go to sporting goods stores and drool (figuratively) over the equipment. I often find myself thinking, "I'd rather be backpacking."

Boy, 17, Virginia

Passions drive a person. Interests are just an escape from serious things. They are more for entertainment and release than passions are.

Girl, 19, Oklahoma

A passion is something you LOVE to do your best at, while an interest is something you LIKE to have fun with. It's good to have both in life, but know the difference. Don't let an interest take away your passion, because passions last longer and are closer to your heart.

Girl, 19, Pennsylvania

## Reflection Connection

Think about a passion in your own life and write about it. How long have you held this passion? How did it start for you? Do you share this passion with anyone, or is it more private? Do you see yourself continuing to pursue this passion as you grow older, or can you imagine other passions taking over? Write as much as you wish about this passion, then put the sheet of paper into an envelope, seal it, and date it. Put the envelope away and don't open it for one year. When you do open it, you may be surprised at what you read.

# Fitting In with Friends and Peers

L ike all other individuals, gifted teenagers are social creatures. Somewhere deep inside of you is the desire to be accepted by others for the person you are.

Everyone has trouble finding acceptance sometimes. But for gifted teens, it can be extra tough. If you are known as the kid in school who always knows the answers to teachers' questions—or who uses an elaborate vocabulary, or who seeks out harder work, or who doesn't seem to care about the same things other teens do—that can have a social consequence. You might be real popular at test-taking time, but your popularity might not continue when the test is over.

Of course, this doesn't mean it's *always* hard for *all* gifted teens to fit in. Lots of gifted teens have no problems maintaining relationships—with gifted *and* nongifted friends. However, if you happen to have peers who are gifted too, and who like some of the same things you do—well, all right! You may have found social nirvana.

## How do your friends react to your abilities? What do friends do or say that makes you feel good or bad about being gifted?

My friends think I'm smarter than I really am, which can be stressful. I feel bad when they don't understand something, because sometimes I don't, either.
Boy, 13, Colorado

Because I am in the gifted program, my friends look up to me. It is as if I am their role model.
Girl, 13, Texas

My friends just see me as one of the guys, only a lot smarter and with a bigger vocabulary.
Boy, 13, New Jersey

I surround myself with other people who are smart. We all try to push each other forward, with interesting science, literature, and political debates at the lunch table. There's a plethora of inside jokes that encourage our individual passions. Our lunch table bursts out laughing at any mention of the words "mononucleosis," "tourism," or "socioeconomic." We're in this together.
Girl, 13, New Jersey

Occasionally I get the odd "Dang it, Devon, stop being smart!" Actually, they're really just teasing me when I get something they don't.

Girl, 13, Texas

My friends treat me different just because I'm in a gifted program. They like saying rude and dumb jokes about my abilities. No one should get made fun of just because they are smart.

Boy, 14, Texas

"My best friends are all gifted and weird. We know it and love it."

I guess I am pretty lucky to have such great friends who don't make fun of me because I am smarter than they are. They just say "Good job, Joe" when I do something at a high education level.

Boy, 14, California

I try not to let the fact that people think I am gifted affect my social life. I want to be like my friends, just another person, because being different sets you apart. Anyone who is different gets laughed at.

Girl, 14, Oklahoma

They make me feel good when they say that I'm smarter in school, but bad when they say I'm dumber in basketball.

Boy, 14, Iowa

My best friends are from the private school for the gifted that I went to during middle school. We're all gifted and weird. We know it and love it.

Girl, 14, Illinois

Sometimes, a phone call that begins "Hi, can you explain the science homework?" leaves me feeling like I have a big sign on my back claiming that I don't want friends, just questions.

Girl, 14, Massachusetts

Most of the time my friends just say, "Why are you so smart?" I really don't like it that I make them jealous.

Boy, 14, Kentucky

Since I have been in college since I was 12, my classmates either ignore me or are nice. No one has been unkind to me since I started at the university. Over the past three years, I have almost started believing again that people can be nice.

Boy, 15, North Carolina

For the past eight years, I have been trying to make people understand that I have the same kinds of feelings and needs as other kids my age. Yet, people continue to think I am "beyond that."

Girl, 15, Kansas

Friends turn to me for help in school, and I don't feel good about them cheating off me sometimes.

Girl, 15, Pennsylvania

I will continue to be a teenage girl, with teenage girl thoughts and feelings, no matter how smart they say I am.

Girl, 16, Kansas

Most of the people I consider friends are from Internet chat rooms. It is one of the few places where the jokes and chat go fast enough to keep me interested.

Boy, 16, Virginia

I don't like it when my friends say "You did an awesome job" when I put about 5 percent effort into it.

Boy, 16, Indiana

Most of my friends don't care one way or the other. When I was younger and had imaginary friends, if one of them started making fun of me, I'd just get rid of him.

Boy, 16, Tennessee

My friends don't really say anything about my being gifted. It's just who I am. When they do say something it's usually to tell me to shut up and stop getting all the answers right when a teacher asks a question.

Girl, 16, Ohio

People make fun of you when your intelligence exceeds theirs because people fear what they do not understand.

Boy, 16, California

My friends are other gifted students, so they don't mind my being smart at all. We talk about whatever is on our minds, rather than boys or current gossip.

Girl, 16, Illinois

Up until the past few years, when I learned to mask my intelligence, I was often made fun of and singled out in many situations.

Boy, 17, Tennessee

"When the pressure was on, there was some resentment toward me. Usually, it was good-natured teasing, but sometimes, the good nature would disappear."

There are times when it's embarrassing to have your friends bring up how intelligent you are. When you're a teenager, all you want to do is fit in, so when being gifted makes you different, you try to shy away from it.

Boy, 17, Michigan

All of my friends are incredibly gifted themselves. We hang out at a coffeeshop drinking iced tea, discussing philosophy, and playing bridge. This isn't elitism, it's just who we relate to.

Boy, 17, Virginia

A lot of my friends are at the same level I am, so it usually becomes a competition to see who can do the best. My friends who aren't in honors courses make me feel bad about being able to pick things up so quickly. Usually, I end up teaching them the material, which makes me feel good, because I can use what I have been blessed with to help others.

Girl, 19, Oklahoma

I was always the one who was gifted without trying to be. So, when the pressure was on, there was some resentment toward me. Usually, it was good-natured teasing, but sometimes, the good nature would disappear.

Girl, 19, North Carolina

When I'm around other gifted people, it's a totally different atmosphere that tends to really lift me up.

Girl, 19, New York

# In Their Words:
# Yuval, Age 17

I've spent my school career in two countries, the United States and my native Israel. I am the youngest of three, and both of my older brothers are serving in the Israeli military, something that is required for both men and women. My name, Yuval, means "little river" in Hebrew. It's an uncommon name in America, but not where I live now, in Hod HaSharon, Israel.

I was like a transatlantic ping-pong ball for my education, attending school in Israel until second grade, coming to the United States for third through fourth grades, returning home for grades five through ten, and returning to America for grade eleven (such is the life of someone whose mom is a doctoral student in the States!). I'm back in Israel now, where I will finish my high school education. I'm not sure what I'll do next: perform my three-year obligation in the army or attend college first and then serve my military duty.

There are differences and similarities in the schools of both nations. One major difference is that in Israel extracurricular

⟶

activities (like marching band) are not offered as a part of school. One similarity is cliques: cliques exist in both countries.

Cliques have always been what they still are today: a social divide. It's almost like school cliques are one big pizza—one slice is "cheerleader," another is "jock," and yet another slice is "book-worm" or "nerd." I'm generally against this system, as I believe it makes people narrow their horizons and have very thin views on subjects and people. One of the things I liked most about moving between two countries was that my views on many subjects broadened greatly. When you hear, and actually listen to, many different views, you eventually have to make up your own mind. This helps to make you a thinking person—an individual.

Before I moved to the United States for the first time, I unknowingly belonged to one of those cliques I claim to dislike! I was one of the "cool boys" in Israel, good at soccer and many other activities deemed to be popular. At age 8 I came to America, where I was an unknown, and I was able to see social divisions from an outsider's point of view. I learned first-hand that it is tough on the "new kid" to find his place when cliques are so, so present. And I did not speak English so, of course, things were difficult for me to understand—I would communicate my needs through gestures! (Still, I learned the language quickly and was fluent within a year.) I actually came to feel ashamed that I was once the boy who didn't want to talk to you because you couldn't play marbles well enough. After that I changed my ways.

And then, when I returned to Israel for the first time (for fifth grade), I found that the clique I had been in before no longer acknowledged me. My soccer skills had diminished in my years in America, and because soccer was such a big fad in Israel, I was instantly unpopular. Eventually I managed to fit in again, due to the fact that I wasn't quick to judge other people. But when I came back to America for the second time (for eleventh grade) I had to start all over. It was even harder than before to find new friends. In high school, it is very hard to break the lines of social cliques.

However, one place I found that actually helped me to break these social lines was my gifted programs, in both the U.S and Israel. In my gifted programs, I met new people I might not have met otherwise: intelligent people with interesting ways of thinking and open minds. I have met some of my best friends in gifted programs, and it would have been a shame if I had never met them because we didn't share the same social cliques.

Even though I'm gifted and do well academically, I have a learning disability that mostly affects reading and writing. I never learned the alphabet when other kids did, and it was confusing to me and my friends in my gifted classes that I could find some things so hard. When I realized that my learning disability might hold me back in some ways, I was both angry and sad. I set out to prove that I was going to learn what I wanted when I wanted. I'm pretty sure I'll always have my disability, but I refuse to make excuses like, "I can't learn that because of being LD."

Music doesn't require the same types of skills as do reading and writing, and math is its own kind of language, and I excelled there. In fact, by the end of tenth grade I was already mastering college level mathematics. But my real passion is music. Both of my older brothers are musicians, and my grandparents exposed me to the works of many great composers when I was quite young. From then on, I was hooked. As I listened more, I became intrigued by "combination" forms of music—like what John Williams composed for *Star Wars*.

When I decided to play an instrument, I chose trumpet, because it is used in so many musical styles—classical, jazz, and more. At first I played third trumpet (an orchestral "voice" you don't often hear), and I became intrigued by the "hidden" nature of the instrument's contribution to a composition.

In Israel I met a student in my grade, No'am, through our after-school band. No'am convinced me in eighth grade to do what he had begun: composing, not just performing. Since we have to select two majors in high school (similar to what American students do

→

in college) I tried to combine my love of music with my fascination with physics.

I'm not sure what my future holds professionally—music? physics? math?—but I do hope to have a family someday: a family with three kids (one kid would get too egocentric and four is too many). I am aware that I might pass on my disability to my children and if I do, I'll be able to help and understand them knowing that I have lived through some of the frustrations they will encounter. Then again, I might also pass along my giftedness.

My frequent moves made some things difficult—it's hard to reestablish connections after being away for a year or more—but they have also made me optimistic. My views have broadened, I have learned to adapt in academic and social situations, and I've overcome a lot. Those life lessons will serve me well in the years ahead.

## Do you ever do anything just to go along with the crowd?

No, I don't do things just to go along with the crowd, because if I don't like something I'm not going to pretend I do just to fit in.
Girl, 13, Ohio

I dyed my hair to go along with the crowd, and also because I always wanted to. That's about it, though.
Girl, 13, Oklahoma

Mostly, I am the one that comes up with the ideas, so I am the crowd leader. A lot of people look up to me.
Boy, 13, California

"If you really knew anything about middle school politics, you wouldn't want to go along with the crowd."

If you really knew anything about middle school social politics, you wouldn't want to go along with the crowd.
Girl, 13, Ontario

Yes, I have done things just to go along with the crowd before, because I was tired of being so special, so alone, and I wanted to belong to the big crowd for a while. It never worked very well, though.

Girl, 13, Maine

I guess everyone has to do a certain amount of camouflage just to get by in high school. I don't go along with the crowd so much as I disguise my speech to make it sound somewhat normal (i.e., incoherent). You have to camouflage yourself a little for self-protection.

Girl, 14, Utah

Nope, because I don't have the proper social skills to know what "the crowd" wants.

Boy, 14, Massachusetts

Senseless conformity is a mark of ignorance.

Girl, 14, Wisconsin

"I feel like it's too much effort to try to make others see the way I see."

Yes, I do, mainly because I don't see why not to. My crowd is not the *in* crowd, but I like it.

Boy, 14, New York

I couldn't do that. I have gifted friends and I'm proud to be different. I hate it sometimes, but I wouldn't give it up for the world. I don't rub it in people's faces, but I don't go along with them just for the sake of doing so.

Girl, 14, England

I wish I were invited to parties and, if I were, I might do something considered "irresponsibly adolescent." I sometimes tell my parents that I wish I were an underachieving delinquent, so that when I make a mistake or do something unethical, it wouldn't be such a big deal.

Girl, 15, Indiana

No, I've learned that it's better to do things for myself. The only person I should have to please is myself, and that's my goal in life. If other people want to jump off a bridge, I hope they have fun.

Boy, 15, Texas

When I was younger, I wanted so much to be liked and accepted. Then, as I got older, I realized that I don't want to be like "those people" at all. I am my own person. I speak my opinion, I wear what I want to wear, and I say what I believe. That doesn't mean that my life is any easier or that I've suddenly found my place in the world, but I feel better about me.

Girl, 15, Kansas

I don't think I know who "the crowd" is. Have I ever met "the crowd"? I guess the answer is no, because I have never been with a crowd.

Boy, 15, North Carolina

It can be fun sometimes, pretending to be someone I'm not. It's really rather amusing.

Boy, 16, Indiana

Yes, sometimes I just try to act like everyone else because I feel like it's too much effort to try to make others see the way I see.

Girl, 16, Ohio

Sometimes I do because I am lonely. I need to pretend I like something so I can feel that I have something in common with my friends.

Girl, 16, Pennsylvania

Yeah, I do. You can't just sit back and be stubborn about your beliefs. Adaptation is a part of life.

Boy, 16, Texas

No. I'm at the top of most things I do, and it's me people turn to for leadership a lot of the time, so I don't really have a choice to follow along. Also, I tend to be very independent, and I choose to be alone a lot, so I do not even look for someone to go along with.

Girl, 16, Iowa

Going along with the crowd is never an option.

Boy, 17, Tennessee

No, what I do I choose to do. As Aesop said, "If you try to please everyone, you will please no one." To go along with the crowd serves no purpose but to please everyone else—and I am here to enjoy my life and my choices.

Boy, 17, Tennessee

If I do something to go along with the crowd, it's a carefully considered decision that I make on a case-by-case basis.

Boy, 17, Nebraska

No, not really. I'm just wallpaper. I try not to stick out, because as the ancient Asian saying goes, "The nail that sticks out gets hammered down."

Girl, 17, New York

Not in elementary or middle school, but in high school I became more concerned about social acceptance, but not to the extent that I would do things against my morals.

Girl, 19, Connecticut

# Reflection Connection

Poet e.e. cummings wrote, "To be nobody but yourself in a world which is doing its best to make you everybody else means to fight the hardest human battle ever and to never stop fighting." Write about a time in your life when you had to stand up for your convictions against tremendous social odds. What price did you pay? Was it worth it? Would you do it again?

# How are you the same as and different from other people your age?

I think the biggest thing I have in common with other children my age is that adults only take me seriously when it is convenient to do so. Sometimes it's hard to talk with other kids, though, because I find myself jumping from Harry Potter to telekinesis to quantum physics, for I find that every subject presents twenty tangents to go out on. I imagine that's hard for other kids to keep track of.

Girl, 13, Pennsylvania

I am a 13-year-old girl. I talk about guys, clothes, fashion. But not on a superficial level. Guys are my best friends, clothes are made to keep us comfortable, and fashion is nonexistent. And people wonder why we don't fit in . . .

Girl, 13, Ontario

They don't always get my jokes. They're like, "Huh? I don't get it!"

Boy, 13, Oregon

I'm not different. I'm good at some things, but I'm bad at others. Everybody has strengths and weaknesses. I may not be average, but I'm not extraordinary, either.

Boy, 14, Massachusetts

I think that my peers don't use their brains too much. They don't seem very curious about the world and are not interested in pursuing further investigation on topics discussed in school. For example, they don't care about philology, yet after watching *The Fellowship of the Ring* I found some Web sites and started learning Sindarin Elvish.

Girl, 14, New Jersey

Many people don't shout out or express feelings like I do. But I'm the same as others with the kinds of feelings I have. I go through the same difficulties and pressures as others.

Girl, 14, Texas

I am different from other kids my age in many ways. One of them is that I am not shy and I am not afraid to go in front of the class and talk or present something. Another thing is that I can hold a conversation with an adult over anything interesting.

Boy, 14, Indiana

I'm really different from people my age. They all judge people for some reason while I see nothing to judge them by.

Girl, 14, Connecticut

I tend to have a deeper understanding of abstract ideas. Many children my age are into sports, music, and other activities that I am interested in, but they have many different tastes that I find somewhat stupid, such as listening to rap music and idolizing the people that influence younger children and corrupt them.

Boy, 14, Ohio

I think I am a little too pensive, too intense, for some people.

Girl, 14, Wisconsin

Because I am surrounded by people who are older than I am (I'm in a higher class than kids my age), I feel the need to always be responsible so I can fit in. Socially, I try to be the same as everyone else, though age differences (and, thus, a driver's license) inhibit this. Academically, though, I usually keep my abilities discreet so that I am not put in the spotlight or made fun of.

Girl, 15, Indiana

I am on the brink of independence and struggling with my place in the world, just as my classmates are, even if we cope with it in different ways. In short, we are adolescents, and as such, must bind together, since the rest of society has just cause to avoid us.

Boy, 15, Massachusetts

One thing that sets me apart from my peers is motivation. Many of the kids around me simply don't care about the future. I, however, know that I want to succeed, and I have plans on how to achieve my goals. Also, I tend to appreciate the arts and literature more than my peers. I love watching plays and old movies, where most kids my age get bored.

Girl, 16, Michigan

I have found that I do tend to think more outside the box, and ask more complex questions than many people in my classes. This can come as a disadvantage, because the benefits of an intellectual discussion are lost among these people.

Boy, 16, Ohio

I am a mall rat, music junkie, and phone freak, just like most 16-year-old American girls. I also discuss theories, observations, and ideas with my friends. It is hard to have an interesting conversation with most of my friends, though, because they say I don't make sense. But with my gifted friends, they finish my sentences on the same subject.

Girl, 16, Iowa

> "I tend to think more outside the box, and ask more complex questions than many people in my classes."

I am mostly different because I think most people my age are shallow and worry about themselves when there is so much famine and war and other important things to consider in life. They are spoiled and I am not. In school, I do not participate in some classes because the students are so uninformed.

Boy, 16, California

I want to learn. Most people don't really even care, but I actually do want to learn. That's not to say I enjoy school and teachers, but I have a desire to learn and understand the world around me.

Girl, 16, Tennessee

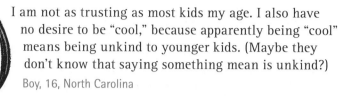

I am not as trusting as most kids my age. I also have no desire to be "cool," because apparently being "cool" means being unkind to younger kids. (Maybe they don't know that saying something mean is unkind?)
Boy, 16, North Carolina

I always feel like I need to educate myself when someone talks about something I don't understand.
Girl, 16, Virginia

I honestly don't know. All of my friends are incredibly smart, and I just don't associate with average kids. It's not any sort of elitism, we just don't have anything in common. I want to discuss philosophy, where they want to discuss MTV. Not a whole lot of crossover . . .
Boy, 17, Virginia

Well, I'm mostly the same in that I like the same clothes, clubbing, rock music, boys, and the rest of that teenage folderol. Sometimes, though, I feel I'm seen as a poser or nerd, in lieu of the cool kid whose persona I affect. My friends tell me I need to chill out, that I am paranoid. It's a feeling I can't shake—the feeling of being a stranger in a strange land.
Girl, 17, New York

I am a teenager before I am gifted, so while I understand certain things at a higher level than the normal student, I am still experiencing many things in the same ways as my friends. I am still going through the late stages of puberty, my mind is still maturing as well as learning, and I still lack many of the skills I shall need for college and beyond. In fact, some of my friends have already taken their positions on adult issues like religion, sexuality, and government that I lack.
Boy, 18, Tennessee

"I think people forget that even if someone is labeled 'gifted' they're still a kid."

I sometimes feel that I catch onto the subtleties of social situations or even world events more quickly than my peers. However, I also am capable of acting just as irrationally as anyone when in certain emotional situations.
Girl, 19, Connecticut

I tended (and still tend) to be more introverted, more thoughtful, and often more cynical than most other kids my age. Other than that, though, I was always a normal kid. I think people forget that even if someone is labeled "gifted" they're still a kid.
Girl, 19, North Carolina

"Although all of my friends are quite brilliant, I'm smarter still. For a long time, I had trouble relating to much of anyone because of this. I had very few social skills and no friends. Eventually, I realized that if I only slept four hours a night, it effectively gave me a partial lobotomy. Although my brain function decreased, I was still one of the smarter people around. I kept myself sleep deprived for a year and a half. In that time, I was able to form friendships. I paid attention to how different people reacted to different things. I learned to take someone who was hostile toward me and turn him into my best friend. In short, I became a social genius.

"About four months ago, I was with a group of people comparable in intelligence to me. I got along with them great, as I could make a friend out of just about anyone I chose to. Unfortunately, I did not take full advantage of this opportunity. Being sleep deprived, I wasn't able to follow the truly complex conversations. I was still able to relate, but it could have been so much more. About a week later, I realized what I was missing out on. That night, I got a full night's sleep, and have almost every night since. Since then, I've actually been more social. Now, I can really pay attention, as opposed to dedicating half my mental energy to trying to stay awake. (As a sidelight, getting only four hours of sleep at night doesn't do much for one's physical appearance—and physical attraction, like it or not, does have something to do with social attraction. Getting enough sleep means I no longer look like a raccoon.)"
Boy, 17, Virginia

# Reflection Connection

Do you behave differently around gifted peers or adults than you do around other peers? Do you think that is appropriate because different situations call for different behavior, or do you see it as "selling out" because you have to become "fake" in order to be accepted by one group of individuals?

## What is it like when you feel smarter than some of your friends?

Sometimes I wish I was just a normal kid, one who liked to hang out with other girls, who thought that dressing in something fashionable and being well-liked was almost as important as getting good grades. I'd like to live just one day to see what living that life would be like.

Girl, 13, Texas

It gets aggravating having to explain a joke to my friends more than once. By then, all the fun has gone out of it.

Boy, 13, Florida

If one of my friends says something about me being smarter than them, I just shrug it off and point out something I think they are really good at.

Girl, 13, Maine

In first grade, I was sitting on the rug coloring with some other kid. All of a sudden, I turned to the kid and said, "You know, I may not exist. You could just be crazy and think I exist." The other kid said, "But you do exist." And I said back, "But I might not." Then, the kid got nervous and told the teacher, and the teacher told me to stop scaring the other kids.

Girl, 13, Massachusetts

If your "friends" don't like you because you are smart, then they were never really your friends in the first place.
Boy, 13, Nebraska

It is really hard at times. Some people pretend to be your friend, but you find out later that all they really want are the answers to homework and stuff.
Girl, 13, Texas

Being gifted doesn't change the fact that I'm still a normal kid, and actually, sometimes I can be quite stupid.
Boy, 14, Utah

Sometimes my friends look up to me, while other times they just mock my smartness.
Boy, 14, Pennsylvania

It's hard when I see my friends make mistakes that I wouldn't make, and then start to automatically correct them. I have to tell myself, "They're not like you. They don't know what you know. Let them learn in their own way." Can I please express how utterly frustrating this is?
Girl, 14, Australia

I realized that if your friends aren't as witty or as intelligent as you are, your conversations are much more shallow. Thus far in high school, I have made friends with more juniors and seniors than freshmen because we are all at the same thought and maturity levels.
Boy, 14, Ohio

"Some people pretend to be your friend, but you find out later that all they really want are the answers to homework and stuff."

I am not in all honors classes. Sometimes my friends are like, "You're not in all honors classes???" When I say no, they are always surprised.

Boy, 14, Ohio

It's nice being recognized, but I wish they would understand that I'm not any different from the average teenager, outside of my thought processes. I still have little experience in the real world, just like them.

Girl, 15, Iowa

When I was younger, it was very frustrating to me to interact with kids my own age because it seemed like they were from another planet. They acted like babies to me. My teachers used to tell me not to use words the other students couldn't understand. I can only hope that my giftedness will pay off in whatever career I choose after college.

Girl, 15, Indiana

Sometimes I feel like I make others think that I am smarter than they are when I don't mean to portray that idea at all. I intimidate them when I don't mean to.

Girl, 16, Minnesota

A lot of times, my age peers can be really shallow and immature. I just try to remind myself that they're at a different place than I am, mentally and developmentally. I have fun with them at their level, but I feel unfulfilled a lot when there is nobody at my level to relate to.

Boy, 17, Kansas

I find that I'm always explaining things two or three ways before people understand what I'm trying to say. Fortunately, nobody ever notices this. Also, I've learned not to cut people off, even though I already know what they're saying. People get offended and feel like you're either not listening to them or patronizing them.

Boy, 17, Virginia

It all kinda evens out sooner or later. By high school, some friends are smarter, some friends are not as smart, and you develop different areas of expertise. Being smarter than my friends is not how I think about it at all.

Girl, 18, Kentucky

Many gifted students mistakenly believe that if others do not have their knowledge they are someone "lesser." An artist does not know the musical repertoire of a pianist, and neither may know the plays of a football jock, but I have personally been in the same math class with all three types.

Boy, 19, Tennessee

# Reflection Connection

Do you think girls or boys have an easier time fitting in at your school? Why do you think that is? What distinct social challenges does each gender face? What social expectations (stated or unstated) does each gender face? Are there perceived **limits** to what either gender can do, academically or socially? Finally, if the individuals we're talking about are gifted, does that change which gender has an easier time fitting in? Why or why not? What factors other than giftedness and gender play into social acceptance at your school?

# Dealing with Expectations—From Others AND Yourself

I f you are gifted, big expectations often come with the territory. You might feel them from parents, teachers, or others who (for just one example) remind you that every B is a strike against you in your quest to get into a top college. Or maybe you feel them from yourself, because your standards are set so high that anything less than perfect is unacceptable. Either way, the gifted label tends to carry the baggage of super-high standards for accomplishment.

There's nothing wrong with having high standards—the pursuit of excellence is certainly healthy—but perfectionism is not. Pursuing excellence is wanting to excel in areas of strength or talent. Excellence lets you shine. But perfectionism is feeling you have to be the best at *everything* you do. If you're a perfectionist, you feel like a loser if you don't come out on top.

As you read this chapter, think about your own academic and personal expectations. For example, would you rather take an easy class because you are assured of getting an A (while learning little), or would you challenge yourself by taking a harder class where an A was not guaranteed? For another example, if you've never ice skated for fear that you'll fall (you will) and make a fool of yourself (you won't), would you take the risk and go skating to see if you like it?

Expectations—from others and yourself—can put a lot of pressure on you. That kind of pressure can lead to loneliness or sadness. See if you recognize any of your own thoughts or feelings in the quotes in this chapter.

## What do you expect from a person with your abilities?

Being gifted may be a blessing and all, but gifted students and adults have their off days too. Even if we're up and running most of the time, we all need a break once in a while.

Girl, 13, Nebraska

I don't expect much from "a person with my abilities." I *would* expect good grades like A's and B's, but if they get a C, I'd understand as long as they tried their hardest. If they didn't try their hardest, then I wouldn't understand the C.

Boy, 13, New York

I expect gifted kids to be reasonable people.

Girl, 13, Indiana

To have very ambitious dreams and to try to be somebody who can affect the world in a good way.

Boy, 13, Iowa

I expect gifted people to be interesting to talk to and be around. I'm almost never disappointed.

Girl, 14, Texas

In terms of pure expectations, I expect someone with my abilities to be more introspective and studious, although I know that isn't always the case. I expect deep interest in several areas, and a bit of idealism.

Girl, 14, Massachusetts

I think people with my abilities should be a cut above the rest. I think they should be more serious and less goofy.

Boy, 14, Ohio

Nothing. Ability is only one factor; attitude and circumstances are required to determine action.

Boy, 14, Georgia

People with "my abilities" are still kids. Yeah, they will seem smart when they do what they are good at doing, but we still need hobbies and friends and stuff like that. There are some things for which studying does not suffice.

Girl, 14, Connecticut

Perfection, with the normal amount of effort. I'm trying to stop thinking this, but I can't.

Girl, 14, England

**"I expect a persistent thirst for knowledge and challenge."**

I expect that they should be able to explain things to me, so that I can learn something.

Boy, 14, Iowa

I expect that people with my abilities won't goof off when it's time to work.

Girl, 14, Ohio

I expect good etiquette from a gifted person, and I expect a persistent thirst for knowledge and challenge.

Boy, 15, Indiana

I don't expect anything from "a person with my abilities." If people are smart, and they choose not to use their abilities, then so be it. People should be allowed to make their own decisions and not be pressured into doing something they don't want to do just because they are "smart."

Girl, 15, Utah

I expect a person with my abilities to always be reaching for that next rung on the ladder. However, this should only go so far. You shouldn't be expected to be stressed out all the time. Nonetheless, I feel that way quite often.

Girl, 15, Iowa

I expect to fulfill my potential . . . but I don't know what that is yet, because my choices are unlimited.

Boy, 16, California

I expect to develop my abilities. I expect to think hard and deeply about things. I expect to feel some sense of loneliness and isolation.

Boy, 17, Kansas

I don't really expect anything. There are all sorts of gifted people and some react badly to being gifted, while others react well. So, I don't really expect anything.

Girl, 18, Virginia

I stopped expecting anything as I met more and more gifted people. There's a whole range of them out there, who cover the entire spectrum on just about any topic you can come up with. In essence, they're just people.

Girl, 19, Kansas

# Reflection Connection

Complete the following statements honestly and, when finished, ask a trusted friend, teacher, or mentor to do the same. Compare your responses and talk about what they mean.

- When I get an A in school . . .
- Most of my friends expect me . . .
- When report cards are issued . . .
- I do best in school when . . .
- When I get a compliment about my work . . .
- No one expects me to . . .
- When I consider my future . . .

If you like, create your own sentence stems and respond to them. Invite that same trusted friend, teacher, or mentor to do the same.

## What do others—adults or friends—expect from you?

My parents expect perfect grades and a perfect personality. If I do this, I get a clap on the back. If I don't, I get questioned about why I didn't.
Girl, 13, Australia

They over-expect me, if there's a word like that.
Boy, 13, Wisconsin

Often, they expect me to be super-organized, which I'm not. (Sometimes, organization is the bane of discovery.)
Girl, 13, Pennsylvania

I don't want teachers putting me down for something minor just because I am supposed to be a role model.
Boy, 13, Ohio

My dad says that I'm sure not gifted at the things in life that matter, like cleaning up and staying organized. He doesn't expect anything more from me because I'm gifted, but he does expect more because I am the oldest sibling.

Boy, 13, Colorado

My parents expect me to help my younger sister with her homework when they don't understand it themselves.

Girl, 13, Nebraska

Ugh. So many people expect me to be able to do things that are just plain out of the ordinary. My parents will hand me logic puzzles or brain teasers and just expect me to solve them. They expect me to do things that are beyond my capability, and then look at me like I'm stupid when I can't solve the problem.

Girl, 14, Connecticut

My friends expect me to act older than everyone else.

Boy, 14, Iowa

"They over-expect me, if there's a word like that."

My mom and dad are just Mom and Dad. They're proud when I'm successful and encouraging when I fail. My teachers expect me to be full of ideas when I enter their rooms.

Girl, 14, Florida

Most people expect way too much. They ask for a lot that I may not be able to provide, and sometimes they even make assumptions about my personality due to my giftedness.

Boy, 14, Kentucky

This is probably the most annoying aspect of life. EVERYONE thinks, "Oh, she's so smart and she knows everything." Does it have to be EVERYTHING? I am not all knowing!

Girl, 14, New Jersey

My parents do not expect as much from me because I have had older siblings who were intelligent, so they trust in the fact that I will not make stupid mistakes and throw my life away. When other adults encounter the fact that I'm gifted, they drop most of the teenage stereotypes and ask me questions about what I like.

Boy, 14, Ohio

I have a strong suspicion that some adults are intimidated by gifted children. I have been belittled and had my opinions undervalued because of my age. Other adults expect from us exceptional "maturity," the word in this context meaning that we will follow any order, head down and mouth shut, not having the foolish audacity to challenge our omniscient elders. I have utmost respect for adults who are wise enough to value my opinions and ideas without discrimination.

Girl, 14, Wisconsin

When I was little, like 3 or 4, people would tell me I would be the first scientist on Saturn or would invent a cure for cancer. That was really hard for me, because I thought I had to accomplish all these things they expected of me. Once my parents figured out how hard it was for me to hear these words, they got people to stop saying things like that, which helped a lot.

Boy, 15, North Carolina

They expect too much. Far too much. I am expected to be the responsible one, the one who knows better, the one who always gets the right answer. I can't be that person. I make mistakes—that's how the world works.

Girl, 16, Kansas

Why am I supposed to be better behaved than other 14-year-olds?

Boy, 14, Illinois

Others expect me to always give 100 percent, even though they don't themselves. I always have to know the answers, even to things I've never heard of. If I don't, it's scandalous.

Girl, 16, Pennsylvania

Others expect an organized, well-behaved, well-dressed, participating person who acts just the way gifted people are "supposed to," not letting any part of my individual personality come out.

Girl, 16, Wisconsin

My mother expects sporadic bouts of genius followed by moments of incredible idiocy—which often happens. Outside of my gifted program teacher, my other teachers see me as a disappointment (at best) and at worst, they see me as a rebel who must be disciplined at all costs.

Boy, 16, Iowa

Most people believe I should have the answer to every question, make the best grades, and overshadow those around me.

Boy, 17, Tennessee

I always have pressure to succeed—to fit into that "doctor/lawyer" mold.

Girl, 17, New York

I honestly think I could walk up to anyone who knows me well and announce that I'd discovered a cure for cancer, and they wouldn't be surprised.

Boy, 17, Virginia

I got my first zero on a homework assignment that I had actually done, due to my not understanding the teacher's instructions. My mother hung this paper on the refrigerator and we all got a good laugh out of it.

Girl, 19, Texas

My mom always says, "If you're so smart, why do you act so dumb?" I know she's not calling me dumb, but nevertheless, this comment puts added pressure on me.

Girl, 19, Pennsylvania

"My mother expects sporadic bouts of genius followed by moments of incredible idiocy— which often happens."

Others expect what I expect: that I will earn good grades, do well in college, and be in a position of influence or at the cutting edge of academia in the future.

Girl, 19, Connecticut

# In Their Words:
# Alicia, Age 13

For as long as I can remember, I've been different from most kids. At age 2, I recited the names of dinosaurs, correcting anyone who said them wrong. I read books when I was 3 and was identified as gifted at age 4. By age 5, I had already decided I'd become a doctor or paleontologist when I grew up. Today, I'm still different from most kids.

One of the few typical things in my life is my family. I live in Denver with my parents and three brothers. Each of us has our own talents and hobbies, so no one outshines anyone else. In addition to paleontology, I enjoy art, music, and equestrian vaulting, which is a combination of gymnastics and dance, performed on a horse. Also, I play three instruments and am a member of the Colorado Honor Band.

School for me is . . . different. I attend the Colorado Virtual Academy (COVA), an online school. I work at home where my lessons are posted on my computer. I mostly do ninth-grade work, but I am also taking several advanced high school courses (Latin I and Honors English). Even though I don't go to a brick-and-mortar school, I still have homework, due dates, and grades. The cool thing about COVA is that no one cares how old I am or if I'm ahead of where I ought to be in school.

My passion for paleontology began when I went on a field trip sponsored by the National Science Foundation (NSF). We stopped at several sites of geological or paleontological significance, and after talking with the field trip directors, Drs. Kirk Johnson and Bob Reynolds, they helped me to get into classes at the Denver Museum of Natural History related to geology, fossilization, plate tectonics,

$\longrightarrow$

and topography. These classes were part of the Paleontology Certification Program. To take these classes, you had to be 17 years
old—I was only 7. Kirk and Bob could see I was more than just a
kid interested in dinosaurs, so they arranged for me to take these
courses. The only stipulation was that my mom had to accompany
me to the classes. So I started, mom in tow.

Things didn't always go smoothly. First, the classes were designed
for college students and most took place at night. I did my best to
concentrate and take notes, but it wasn't easy for a 7-year-old to be
in class until 9 p.m. An especially memorable final project for one
course required students to write a scientific paper. Mine was titled
"A comparison of the facial sutures of the Trilobite Orders *Phacops,
Calymene,* and *Ptychopariida.*" I spent several days researching,
writing, and revising. When my project was turned back to me, I
had received a perfect score!

By age 10, I received my certification in the program. To celebrate, my classmates and I camped out for a week at the Elbert
County Fairgrounds where, every day, I experienced what it meant
to be a field paleontologist and geologist, collecting and identify-
ing fossils. That same year, at a banquet, I received my Paleontology Certification. I was proud to have made it so far, happy to have
finished, and excited about what would happen next for me.

Well, it didn't take long to find out. I now volunteer at the Denver
Museum of Nature and Science, interacting
with the public, telling and showing them
what is beneath their feet, and display-
ing fossils and samples from major rock
layers in the Denver Basin. Also, my
fieldwork has continued, as I have
spent several summers
assisting in excavating
a Diplodocus skeleton in
Thermopolis, Wyoming.
This specimen is very
well preserved, but
all tangled up with
itself. There are ribs
twisted completely
around, feet stuck

under legs, and too many bones. It is hard to get one out without finding another in a spot that complicates everything. I am constantly cleaning up rock and dust, so as not to pull apart a fragile bone. This whole project is really like a complex jigsaw puzzle. I often consolidate uncovered fragments with glue (frequently consolidating my fingers, as well!). When a fossil can be brought up, we put a "plaster jacket" on it, which is burlap strips coated in plaster. With any leftover plaster, my colleagues and I have plaster fights to see who can get the most on each other. Very fun! Once the plaster is dry (over the fossil, not the people), the bone can be rolled out or brought out using ropes and platforms. It is thrilling to watch a bone that I have worked on come out of the quarry.

In addition to my fieldwork, I do scientific drawings combining one of my hobbies (art) with one of my passions. I use lead pencils, art pens, and/or colored pencils to draw individual fossils of whole animals. As I draw, it is as if these long-extinct creatures come back to life.

Some people assume that I do much of this advanced work because I am pressured to do so by other people—like my parents— but that is not the case. Even though studying paleontology is not a typical activity for someone so young, I choose to do all these activities for one simple reason: I *love* doing them! My own ever-going cycle of high personal expectations keeps me at my best. Under most circumstances, I know what I need to do to achieve. I make mistakes, just like everyone does, but if I don't feel challenged, I don't learn. For the most part, my mentors understand, although I do hear an occasional, "Just slow down and enjoy your childhood." But to me, that's exactly what I am doing.

There is also the occasional adult who cautions that if I go through my education too quickly, I'll be too young to get a job when I graduate from college. The alternative, though, is sitting through typical high school classes that I really don't need, and that doesn't seem like a good option to me. So, I have accepted that not everyone will understand my need to know, and that's okay. I can't change other people's minds about what I need to do and be, but I do know what I *feel* I need to do and be. I'll continue to hold onto my dreams, despite some outside pressures to let them go.

## How do others react when you make a mistake? How do you react?

When my parents see mistakes, they make me feel like I failed them. What I feel like when I mess up is that I will never be anybody if I keep doing this.

Boy, 13, Iowa

Adults are disappointed when I make a mistake. I just wish they would cut me a little slack sometimes.

Girl, 13, Maine

> "My friends act like Armageddon has just arrived when I mess up. But hey, I'm human too!"

I see my mistakes as learning opportunities—nothing more.

Boy, 13, Ohio

When I make a mistake, some of my friends act sarcastically toward me. However, I have learned that I shouldn't try to correct *their* mistakes, since people say, "Shhh . . . she's gifted and she'll correct you!"

Girl, 13, Texas

I usually only make mistakes due to carelessness. On a test, for example, I get very annoyed and angry if I get a 99 percent when the reason I got something wrong was something stupid or careless.

Girl, 14, New Jersey

I guess I always want to be better than last time, so if I make a stupid mistake I think, "Oh, this is really bad. I'm turning stupid. I am capable of so much better." For that reason, getting a B is very hard for me to accept.

Girl, 14, Illinois

My friends are often amused or, I think, relieved when I do poorly on a test or essay at school. I'd be happier getting average grades than good ones, because it would probably indicate that I am learning something in school.

Girl, 14, Massachusetts

People just think, "Oh my gosh, Little-Miss-Perfect goofed up!" I think, "So what . . . the world still moves on."
Girl, 14, Utah

What gets me mad is when I see someone my age or younger get something right and I get it wrong. I get so mad because I feel like I should know what they already do.
Girl, 14, Texas

My friends don't really react when I make a mistake. They make a joke about it and then we burst out laughing.
Boy, 14, Iowa

My friends act like Armageddon has just arrived when I mess up. But hey, I'm human too!
Boy, 14, Texas

Ever since I was labeled as gifted, a great deal of stress has been placed on me. This, in turn, has turned me into something of a perfectionist, which is why I hate making mistakes.
Boy, 14, California

Adults, I think, sometimes wish they were as smart as me, so when I fail, they react in two different ways: either they rub it in my face and continue to remind me about this failure, or they are super supportive while laughing inside at me.
Girl, 16, Indiana

My parents get pretty mad when I make a low B. (I guess they'll be unpleasantly surprised today— it's report card day.)
Boy, 16, Tennessee

When I make a mistake, I'm probably harder on myself than anyone else is on me. My friends almost gloat about it when they see I've faltered, and that hurts.
Girl, 16, New York

When I make a mistake, my own reaction usually depends on how big it is. Usually, if I just get something wrong, I just feel embarrassed, but if someone else remarks upon it, it will ruin my entire day.

Girl, 16, Wisconsin

I used to get really frustrated and embarrassed. Other people seemed not to care, but I thought they did. Now, I just put another mark in my column of experience.

Girl, 18, Virginia

I am my toughest critic. I constantly feel that I could do better, but I am constantly tempered by the idea that wishing won't make it so.

Boy, 18, Tennessee

Nonacademic situations, like sports and music, have taught me that it's okay to make mistakes.

Boy, 18, Utah

It's okay to make mistakes. The important part is to learn why the mistake was made and how to fix it.

Girl, 18, China

When I was younger, there were a lot of things I would refuse to do for fear of making a mistake and looking stupid in front of others. Even now, there are times when I won't speak out in class for fear of being wrong.

Girl, 19, North Carolina

## Reflection Connection

Some gifted students love challenges, and others avoid them at all costs—especially if a grade is involved. What about you? Do you prefer the security of tasks where you know you'll succeed, or do you crave the challenge of attempting something new, foreign, mysterious, or difficult?

To help you find out, create a "comfort inventory," a list of several different risks and an evaluation of how comfortable you are taking each one. Include physical, intellectual, social, and emotional risks. An example of a physical risk would be to try a sport or game that is new to you. An intellectual risk could be to take a college-level course while in high school. A social risk could be to stick up for yourself or for a peer who is picked on. An emotional risk could be to share your feelings with someone who might not expect to hear them. Compile your inventory by recalling decisions you made recently in each of these areas, then rate your comfort on a scale of 1 (totally uncomfortable) to 5 (no problem).

Once you've completed your list, determine which category (or categories) you are most comfortable taking risks in, and which ones leave you queasy. This may or may not change the way you make decisions about risk in the future, but understanding why you make those decisions can help you be more self-aware.

## Can a person overachieve?

Those who overachieve are the ones who like to finish work about a week in advance. Their work must be the greatest and done to the fullest. An overachiever can sometimes take on too many things and still expect them all to be completed in a second— *everything* has to be their absolute best.

Boy, 13, Texas

One thing that annoys me is the kid who always has his hand up yelling "OOO! OOOH!" Now *that* kid is an overachiever.

Boy, 13, Minnesota

No, a person cannot overachieve. I believe that if you set your goals high, you will go much further in life. Always remember that to get where you want to go you need a little bit of gas and a lot of knowledge. (That's my mom's philosophy. She's not a philosopher, but I think she's a very smart woman.)

Girl, 13, Ohio

There are some kids in our gifted program who will start to cry or get mad if they get a 95 on a paper. These kids need to calm down and not worry so much. Not many good things come out of overachieving.

Boy, 14, Kansas

I think a person can overachieve when they always study and stay up all night to do extra work. When you just try your best and spend a little more time perfecting your work, that's okay.

Girl, 14, New Jersey

When someone tries extra hard on a simple assignment, that's overachievement. Also, when people write essays with big words instead of simple ones and creative ones, that's overachievement.

Boy, 14, Iowa

I have a friend of average intelligence who tries to overachieve to make herself seem smarter. She color codes her notes and is always working toward extra credit. Even though she is not that smart, she makes excellent grades.

Girl, 15, Indiana

"You can achieve more than you had planned, but this is not overachievement. I think 'overachievement' should be deleted from the English language."

I suppose they can. They can stretch themselves too thin and run themselves without all the pieces that they need to be complete.

Girl, 15, Australia

I do not believe a person can overachieve. You can achieve more than you had planned, but this is not overachievement. I think "overachievement" should be deleted from the English language and no longer be used in public schools.

Boy, 15, Pennsylvania

As a gifted student and something of a perfectionist, I face pressure from myself and others to do better than I ever have before . . . to always do better. If I do badly on a homework assignment or a quiz, I wonder how this is possible if the class is so easy, and I think that I must be turning stupid. For me, every improvement means almost nothing; it just supports what I already know. But every bad grade makes me think that I am becoming a failure. How else do I respond to this than to overachieve?

Girl, 15, Illinois

Yeah, if someone does so much that it gets too stressful for them, or if they do things just because grades are the only thing they really care for, not people or hobbies, that is overachieving.

Boy, 15, Connecticut

No one can overachieve. Overachievement is a term created by lazy people.

Girl, 16, Ohio

No! I don't think there is such a thing as overachievement. "Overachievement" means that you did more than you are capable of doing—but if you did it, you are capable of it!

Boy, 16, Colorado

I understand the meaning of overachievement, but at the same time, how does that even make sense? To achieve is to perform or carry on with success, so if you are capable of doing that, how can that be "too much" accomplishment?

Girl, 16, Alabama

Yes, people overachieve when they spend so much time on work that they fail to remember that things other than their own goals exist in life.

Boy, 17, Tennessee

# Can Your School Keep Up with You?

I t's no secret that school can be frustrating for gifted kids. It's hard to stay interested and motivated when you aren't challenged. And there are lots of reasons gifted kids don't get challenged in school. Students with a wide range of abilities share the same classrooms, so teachers sometimes feel it's necessary to focus on the average kids and kids who have problems learning. Standardized tests are given with increasing frequency, so teachers may feel limited in the subject matter they can teach (some choose to "teach to the test"). And educators often play many roles—teacher, counselor, coach, and comrade—so their time and energies are stretched thin.

But many schools do work for gifted kids. In our experience, schools that work best for gifted students provide something *different,* not just something *more.* For example, "something more" might mean doing the same work as everyone else and then having the "privilege" of doing additional work on top of that. But "something different" might mean eliminating the work you already know and replacing it with material that is challenging and engaging. When gifted students find a learning environment that taps into their talents—and a teacher who respects their abilities—they know they have struck gold, educationally speaking. And they're grateful for this chance to shine. When they can't find such a learning environment, school can be a frustrating place.

It's unrealistic to expect each minute of every school day to hold the excitement of a Steven Spielberg blockbuster, but it is perfectly reasonable to expect your academic and creative needs to be met—or at least addressed. You deserve to be challenged. (Some families with gifted kids feel home-schooling is their best option.)

So what makes schools work for gifted students? What needs to change or improve if gifted students are to enjoy the full benefits of a strong education? That's what we wanted to know.

## Describe your typical school day.

In a typical school day, I'm usually rushing to get to my next class. Once I'm there, if I'm not learning something new, it can get pretty boring (but my classes are usually fun). I usually get plenty of time to socialize between classes. At day's end, I just load up my backpack with homework and head for the bus.

Girl, 13, Iowa

On a typical school day, I learn many different things just so that I can get tested on them later to see if I was paying attention.

Boy, 13, Nevada

A typical day has me going to the gifted class and then two other classes before chorus. In chorus, I get picked on because I am smart and a little overweight. Then, lunch, recess, some more teasing, and the last three classes of the day. Finally, I ride the bus home with everyone screaming their heads off.

Girl, 13, Ohio

"My typical day is filled with frustration with other people's learning pace."

A typical school day finds me sitting in class listening to the teacher explain the assignment and then doing it. Turning in homework and talking with friends rounds out the typical day.

Girl, 14, Texas

On a typical day I just go to classes and do my work. Sometimes I have interesting conversations with people I don't know.

Boy, 14, Texas

Thirty-five minutes of boredom, six minutes of mild interest, and the rest of the period doing anything I can without a) getting into trouble, b) the teacher noticing me, or c) aggravating anyone around me. When I get a subject of mild interest to me, I listen and do the work, getting patted on the head for my seemingly effortless results. In sum, a typical day involves pain, a bit of isolation, and a lot of misery.

Girl, 14, Australia

Typically, I walk into class and an assignment is on the board. The teacher tells you to do it and then gives you your homework. I then just wait for the next class in hopes of getting my day over with soon.

Boy, 15, Colorado

First period: Spanish, which is usually fun, as we sing songs and present skits. English is also fun. In science, the teacher has the most helpless look, as the gifted students write and draw diagrams on the board to better explain or expand upon what the teacher just said. The teacher simply says, "This isn't AP, you know." In social studies, the entire class debates the decisions of the Aztecs. In math, I zone out and mess around with the equations while everyone else is still stuck on the basics.

Girl, 14, New Jersey

On a typical day, I feel pretty tired and lazy. I feel like I don't want to do anything, but I eventually get myself up to do it so that I can get the grade I am working for.

Boy, 15, Michigan

A typical school day is boring and tedious, filled with repetitive work that it seems like we've been studying for years. It involves being forced to work with "partners" where you inevitably have to drag the other person along with you and then wait for them. My typical day is filled with frustration with other people's learning pace.

Boy, 16, Iowa

I go to boring classes that I don't feel are necessary. I get looked down on for raising my hand or knowing answers, so I simply sit there. Then we do group activities where I am stuck with all the work.

Girl, 16, Ohio

A typical day entails time in which I am uninterested in what's going on around me and nothing inspires me to think of anything good to write about.

Boy, 16, Indiana

Fill in the blanks. Write the letter to the correct answer. Complete the crossword puzzle. Ugh.

Boy, 17, Wisconsin

## Describe your perfect school day.

On a perfect day, my morning would start by meeting and talking with friends about anything and everything. My classes would be smooth rides, and none of my teachers would get on my back for simple, little things. For lunch, there'd be something delicious (none of that gross pizza), and then I'd return to classes that involve getting up and conversing, while having to think about what's going on in the work we get to do.

Girl, 13, Texas

A perfect school day is having no one pick on a kid who is not as fortunate as others. Also, a perfect school day would be when we have a snow day and get out early (without homework, of course).

Girl, 13, Iowa

A perfect school day would be going to school and playing and talking with my friends. Then, we would have challenging work in all our classes.

Boy, 13, Texas

A perfect school day is walking in and finding a sub who does not know there was homework to turn in.

Girl, 13, Texas

A perfect day would occur when I don't have to be the one to get the highest grade on a test or when someone gives a better answer than I can.

Boy, 13, Nevada

A perfect school day is when I get to move between as many or as few subjects as I would like to explore and I get to do challenging work that is not simply handed to me on a platter.

Girl, 13, Australia

Perfect days only occur on the last day of school.

Boy, 14, North Carolina

During a perfect school day, I would be treated like everyone else.

Boy, 14, Washington

A perfect day is when the classrooms are calm and small—at least half the class is gone somewhere else. Then, there is a feeling that you can actually learn. To me, a perfect school day is fresh and small.

Girl, 14, Arizona

A perfect school day would go by quickly and involve no homework, leaving me time for a long bath until I fall asleep reading.

Girl 15, Iowa

A perfect school day would include classmates who were kind, teachers who enjoyed working with me, and getting to learn at least one thing that is new and interesting.

Boy, 15, North Carolina

Perfect school days occur when I learn new things, complete my homework during class, feel good about my appearance (which I sometimes have issues with), and have some people to talk with.

Girl, 15, Indiana

Being able to finish off the school day and still be in a good mood would be a perfect school day for me.

Boy, 15, Minnesota

When we do group activities and actually learn something new as we bounce ideas off of one another, that's a perfect school day.

Girl, 16, Ohio

Get there on time, not get embarrassed in any way, open my locker with ease, and have Mr. Mac as my sub in chemistry (he's the *best* sub!).

Girl, 16, Pennsylvania

In a perfect school day, the teachers would ask you what you want to learn and then provide the resources for you to do just that. Then, you would discuss your work directly with the teacher. Also, you could spend as much time on a topic as you want to.

Boy, 16, Pennsylvania

Perfect: write an essay on what you feel about a topic important to you, look under the microscope and draw a picture of the organism, and read to your heart's content.

Boy, 17, Wisconsin

Many students comment that teachers make school interesting by making it "fun." What does "fun" schoolwork mean to you? Does fun imply playing Twister to learn vocabulary or jumping up and down on elevators to see the effects of force on a body? Or does fun mean lessons that are spiced with hands-on activities? Does it mean being introduced to challenging new ideas and resources? Does it mean time to explore your own interests? Can learning be interesting without being fun?

## What are the biggest challenges in school for gifted students?

Dealing with teachers who run away from extremely bright children is my greatest school challenge. Teachers should embrace students like these rather than try to form them into a seventh grade stereotype. The next biggest challenge is to find students who can really be friends with me. Most kids my age are into how tight their jeans are, not the human response to the unknown.

Boy, 13, New York

The biggest challenge for gifted students is simply to get through each day at school. I know that gifted classes are nothing to joke about, but some teachers give us way too much work and have very high expectations.

Boy, 13, Texas

We are more pressured to always do well in school and to set a good example for the other students—that's the biggest challenge.

Boy, 13, Kansas

"Most kids my age are into how tight their jeans are, not the human response to the unknown."

I'm a year younger than my grade, and I'm in advanced classes, so when sophomores and juniors see me in their classes, they aren't always as polite as they could be. They say things like, "Wow! You must really be smart!" How do you respond to that? It's impossible.

Girl, 13, Oklahoma

The biggest challenge for me is not to let my grades slip, which is tempting to do, because the work involves things I already know.

Boy, 13, Iowa

The most challenging aspect during school is trying not to impress somebody by doing their work or other things to show them that you are cool. Being a gifted student can put a lot of pressure on you to fit in with others.

Girl, 14, Louisiana

Organization and time management are my biggest challenges.

Girl, 14, New Jersey

The biggest challenge is always having to do better. Say you get a really good grade on a report card. Now you are expected to do just as well or better the next six weeks. That can sometimes be a great task. The six weeks get tougher and tougher but you are still expected to keep up your grades. No one really understands this except the students. "Gifted" might mean we're smart, but we still mess up and need breathing room.

Boy, 14, Texas

The biggest challenge is finding the time to volunteer at causes I know are worthwhile. If you are gifted and believe you can use your gifts to better your community, by all means, get started! It's just finding the time that's so hard.

Girl, 14, Washington

People think we are different and I often get classified as a nerd because I am in the EXCEL Program. They don't understand that it is not *my* choice to be separated from my friends to go to this class.

Girl, 14, Maine

The biggest challenge for me would have to be dealing with other people who always want answers from me. It bugs me so much. Why can't they just use their own talents? I know they could do it. They just don't try.

Boy, 14, Texas

Making friends is tough. Kids are sometimes jealous and like to make fun of smart kids, to cover their jealousy. It hurts sometimes.

Boy, 14, Oregon

"I've been homeschooled since kindergarten. In preschool, I was more interested in daydreaming, pretending, and doing my own thing. I was also the only kid there capable of writing my name, complete with nickname (Buttercup) and middle name. All my teachers and every other adult I came into contact with thought there was something wrong with me and that my mom had to do something to 'fix' me, because I'd be very unhappy in my school career if I didn't change. Well, my mom and I liked me the way I was, thank you very much, and so we decided to homeschool.

"Of course, it helped my learning. I was able to read many adult-level books on whatever topics I was interested in (mainly science), as well as having more time to spend on violin, writing, dancing, and, surprisingly enough, with friends! But the most important part of homeschooling was that I didn't have to feel I had to change myself in order to be accepted by others. I didn't have to face criticism for all the things that were a fundamental part of my personality, and so until fifth grade (when I went to a private school for three years), I was able to be emotionally healthy. I'm very grateful for having been homeschooled.

"I don't think homeschoolers need to be brought back into the system. The fact that they are opting out will cause the public schools to make adjustments or lose students (and money). The reasons I opted out are that in school there is little room for creativity, original thinking, or independent learning. In high school (I spent a year there) I learned almost nothing but was forced to spend hours doing homework on the order of worksheets. I think there should be fewer worksheets and lectures taken directly out of the textbook and more discussion and independent reading, like is done in college."

Girl, 16, Illinois

Right now, I need time to follow my passions of religion and psychology. I want to read novels by Jane Austen, Tolstoy, and Dostoyevsky. I want to write a book for other gifted teenagers on ways we can improve our educational system. I just need time.

Girl, 15, Illinois

My biggest challenge is to not become lazy. I see a lot of my friends who used to make really good grades but now are flunking because they won't do work that is boring to them.

Girl, 15, Colorado

"Kids are sometimes jealous and like to make fun of smart kids, to cover their jealousy. It hurts sometimes."

Everyone knows you as the "smart kid" and nothing else. Being expected to act in a particular way is certainly a challenge.

Girl, 16, Ohio

The biggest challenge is trying to stay focused on the present because we are always thinking of our futures. Losing sight of my childhood is a concern.

Boy, 17, Georgia

Putting up with twelve years of education that we could learn in four years.

Boy, 18, California

# In Their Words:
# Hector, Age 19

Sometimes, life is a series of contradictions. In my case, I am an identified gifted student, yet I have dyslexia. I love books, even though I have always had a hard time reading them. I was an all-star on my middle school football team, but had to stop play-ing in high school due to repeated injuries. Ups and downs: I've lived them both.

I remember preschool as being very boring because I knew every-thing already. I got tested for the gifted program, and the results showed that I was among the top students in the school district. In kindergarten, I pretended to do all the worksheets, filing them away in my folder and then going to the hands-on centers that I loved. My teacher was not happy to learn that I had not finished one worksheet in an entire six-week period.

First grade was a nightmare. Even though I could read words on flashcards (I memorized the shapes of the words), I could not read these same words when they were in sentences or paragraphs; all the letters and words ran together. I even remember doing "mirror writing," so that when I spelled my name it looked something like this: "rotceH." My dyslexia was becoming evident, which led me to my twice-exceptional label of gifted with a learning disability.

The services I received for my dyslexia were really lame. As a first grader, I was plopped in front of a television listening to instructors speak in monotone voices for 45 minutes. My class-room teachers didn't understand me either. One teacher called me to the board to do a math problem and when I wrote some numbers backwards, she walked to the window and pretended to bang her head on the windowpane, out of desperation. I stood there feeling humiliated—now, all of my classmates knew of my problem. I had always told my friends that I was going to classes for super smart kids, but now they thought I was stupid. When I went home and told my mom what happened, she went to see the principal who promised that would never happen again.

In fourth grade, things took a turn for the worse. My home-work assignments were taking me all night to complete, and they all involved an eternal drudgery of dictionary work and senseless worksheets. My gifted teacher called my parents to a meeting and told them that I was not cutting it in her classes due to my time in the dyslexia program. She told my parents to choose one or the other: services for my giftedness or my dyslexia, for I could not have both. My mother insisted on both. (I think her exact words were: "He needs both, and if he doesn't get them, we'll slap you with a lawsuit so fast you won't know what hit you.") The meeting ended abruptly, and I continued to receive dual services.

Around that time, a family friend convinced my parents to let me play football. Even though my mom was against it at first, a priest we knew convinced her it would be a good thing. "He plays, you pray the rosary," he told my mom. She did, and football became a turning point in my life. I played middle linebacker and was voted as Most Valuable Player at the end of my first year. All of a sudden, the negative attention I had been getting for my dyslexia took a back seat to the positive regard I now got from my schoolmates. The following year, I asked to be removed from the dyslexia program, as it was still as lame as ever. Everyone agreed that would be the best solution.

I looked forward to high school. I had always dreamed of the glory attached to walking onto the field on a Friday night, doing what I did best—football. But one day I was helping my dad move a camper in our backyard and I sprained my shoulder. The injury required surgery, forcing me to sit out my freshman year. Following extensive physical therapy, I was able to play football again as a sophomore. But then, the following summer, I was on a deep-sea fishing trip and fell on deck when a big wave hit our boat. Once again, my shoulder got injured, and since we didn't get back to shore for more than eleven hours, the shoulder separation caused much internal bleeding. Surgery was delayed for weeks, and I learned that if this injury were to occur again, I might lose control of my arm. I decided not to risk it, and I resigned myself to the fact that I would never again play the game I loved to play. I cried, I lamented, I got angry . . . and then I got over it. I'm no quitter.

Instead, I became the team trainer, which allowed me to stay close to football. I took an athletic trainer's class, and I learned first aid, CPR, medical terminology, and how to assess injuries and rehabilitate athletes. I volunteered as a trainer for every single sport, and I never stood in the back with the other trainers—I stood on the sidelines with the athletes. It's a habit I never broke.

Little did I know then that becoming an athletic trainer would lead me in my current career direction: sports medicine. I ended up taking courses in science and technology that allowed me to become certified as both a nursing assistant and a phlebotomist, and when I graduated high school—this gifted kid with dyslexia—I was in the top 10 percent of my class, good enough to gain entrance into the highly competitive University of Texas.

My college acceptance letter arrived on my grandfather's birthday. Everyone was proud (yes, my mother cried) that I had been admitted to UT. I would be the first in our family to attend a flagship university. I was Austin bound.

When I arrived on campus, I registered with the Office of Students with Disabilities and, for my first two years, I communicated my special learning needs to my professors. The second semester of sophomore year, though, I decided not to ask for modifications and to just be a regular student—from time to time during my entire school experience, I have gone through periods of just wanting to be "normal."

As I prepare to return to my junior year at UT, with my major in physical therapy, I realize that much of my success is due to my mental stamina and self-confidence. After my two surgeries, I realize the rewards of helping others to regain their strength and get back into the swing of life. Much of the healing is physical, but with the right attitude, it can also be mental, or even spiritual.

## Does being creative ever get in the way of learning at school? Does it ever get you in trouble?

Depending on the individual teacher and curriculum, being creative can work for or against you. Last year, I had the most amazing English teacher. She would just let us write, every day. Everyone in the class had their creative horizons expanded massively. It was then that I first learned the joy of speaking to someone's soul through a form of art. This year has been plagued by standardized testing (PLEASE don't get me started!) and when I took the extra time to incorporate rhythmic motif into my poem, my English teacher scolded me, saying that I should not use rhythmic motif if we have not covered it in class. That hurt me.

Boy, 13, New York

All creativity does is give you new ways to figure out stuff, so it doesn't get in the way. In fact, being creative I find I am a master at getting out of trouble!

Girl, 13, Illinois

"Creative people are forced to choose between creating meaningful things and doing schoolwork. I live to write, but I am forced to choose between doing my homework and writing, because I have no time to do both."

If you are not creative you end up earning better grades. Being creative means making things harder than they have to be.

Girl, 13, Kansas

77

In a sense, being creative gets in the way of school in that creative people are forced to choose between creating meaningful things and doing schoolwork. I live to write, but I am forced to choose between doing my homework and writing, because I have no time to do both. Often, school makes me so tired that when I get home, I have no energy left to create.

Boy, 14, Illinois

Yes and no. If you have a tendency to doodle and not listen when you're drawing, you can get in trouble. But, if you are in art class and you are doodling in a good way, you'll get a high grade.

Boy, 14, Arizona

Creativity only gives me trouble in math. You have to do the problems in a certain way, and when I get the right answer by using another method, I get marked wrong.

Girl, 14, Ohio

In elementary school, I could never pass the timed tests in math, because I was always looking for patterns instead of just solving the problems.

Girl, 14, New Jersey

Creativity only gets in the way when schools follow a very strict curriculum.

Boy, 15, Massachusetts

My creativity helps me in school, during sports. I can break down a defense in basketball by visualizing the whole floor and seeing where the defense is moving. That way I learn how to play against both the opposing team and with my teammates.

Boy, 14, Ohio

Multiple choice tests don't allow for any creativity. Sometimes I just make up my own answer and circle it, because none of the other answers are really good ones. My teachers don't like this.

Boy, 15, Colorado

I am not artistically creative, but I am verbally and socially creative. For example, if I've known you for a little while, I can pick you out the perfect birthday present or mix you an awesome CD. Or, if you give me a topic, I can write a mean essay. And yes, this can get me in trouble at school. I've frequently been criticized for my creativity, most specifically in writing. I have learned to find out the style of each teacher and conform my style to suit what they want in order to earn an A.

Girl, 15, Indiana

In a very structured classroom, thinking outside the box is not appreciated. I have a tendency to question my teachers' teaching styles. I am not afraid to upset them and hold my ground.

Boy, 16, Iowa

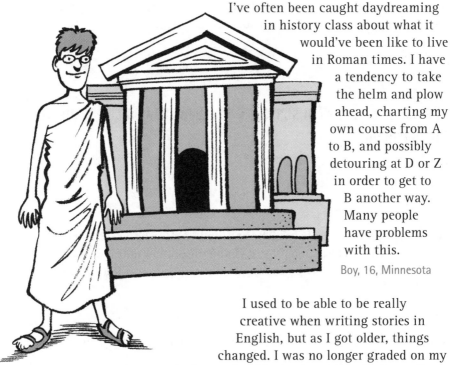

I've often been caught daydreaming in history class about what it would've been like to live in Roman times. I have a tendency to take the helm and plow ahead, charting my own course from A to B, and possibly detouring at D or Z in order to get to B another way. Many people have problems with this.

Boy, 16, Minnesota

I used to be able to be really creative when writing stories in English, but as I got older, things changed. I was no longer graded on my creativity, but on how much the teacher liked my writing. And usually, when a teacher was boring, they didn't like to read things that dealt with fairies or anything else nonhuman.

Girl, 16, Georgia

I believe everyone is creative in their own way, and my way is dance. I want to pursue dance after high school, but no one whatsoever has helped me. In the eyes of my parents and teachers, I'm a dumb little girl who wants to jump around for a living and isn't serious because she's so caught up in her little dream.

Girl, 16, California

Oh yes, creativity can get in the way in school! A lot of times teachers expect one certain answer that they consider the "right" answer. When a gifted individual comes up with a creative answer or solution to a problem, teachers may not take the time to hear you out because they are tied into believing only their own answer.

Girl, 17, Maryland

Sometimes, being creative means you have opinions that can get out of hand, as they are not considered socially or politically correct. Happens to me.

Boy, 17, Tennessee

## Are you ever bored in school? If so, what do you do to relieve the boredom?

I never get bored! The gifted teacher taught us how not to be bored by making up our own stuff to do.

Boy, 13, Oklahoma

When I get bored in class (which isn't often) I start to do some home-work for another class. Sometimes, doing absolutely nothing in class can be fun for some, but for me it gets very boring, so I'll always have a backup plan.

Girl, 13, Texas

I just sit there and pretend to listen in case the teacher calls on me to answer a question.

Boy, 14, California

When I get bored I sometimes tap my pencil or, on occasion, take a ten-minute nap. I don't usually take a nap, but sometimes I can't resist.

Boy, 13, Massachusetts

I write songs really, really small in the language that I've made up or draw in the columns of my notebook—anything that I think will maintain my attention, since the class isn't.

Girl, 14, Connecticut

I think that school does not understand my passion for knowledge. I suppose that's really what it is. For example, we will go over Shay's Rebellion but we won't discuss how the Rebellion set a precedent for citizen political expression. We will discuss Sir Isaac Newton, but we will not examine how he influenced not only science in Europe, but also music, art, architecture, and even literature. I am worried that I will never be stimulated academically until college. (I am sure this is not an uncommon lament.) My older sister says "it will get harder in high school," but I am skeptical. When she says "harder" she means "more work," not necessarily more stimulating work. However, I may be mistaken.

Boy, 14, New York

"My older sister says 'it will get harder in high school,' but I am skeptical. When she says 'harder' she means 'more work,' not necessarily more stimulating work."

I got bored once in sixth grade. My teacher was explaining some math and I fell asleep while he was talking because I already knew what he was talking about. He yelled at me and ordered me to wake up. I did the work and got 100 percent. He got even madder at me that I wasn't paying attention but still got a good grade.

Boy, 14, Utah

A better question to ask is, "Are there ever times when you are *not* bored in school?" The answer? Yes, during music.

Girl, 14, Ontario

I used to be a great student who always did his work, but after a while school got so boring that I just started acting up. School did not (does not) matter to me anymore.

Boy, 14, Texas

If I am starting to get bored, I will ask the teacher if I can go somewhere else and she lets me, since she knows that I finish my work early and that I usually do a great job.

Boy, 14, Louisiana

When I get bored I try to pay attention more, but sometimes it just slips through my hands, so I begin to daydream. Then, I take the book home and read what the teacher read in class, adding little bits of flare here and there.

Girl, 14, Ohio

When I'm bored, I daydream a lot about guys, friends, and just things that are going through my mind that I need to solve. I usually end up getting in trouble for not paying attention.

Girl, 14, Oregon

When school gets less interesting for me, I seem to not pay attention like I should. Then, things start showing up on my grade sheets that I don't like. But when my classes are boring, I can't help it.

Boy, 14, New York

Why do teachers assume at the beginning of the year that we have lost all knowledge from previous years?

Boy, 14, New Jersey

It's always "been there, done that." It hasn't been so bad this particular semester, but in the first half of the year I quite literally thought I was going to die of apathy and sluggishness, brought on by lack of mental exercise. The only way I survived was through constant writing and constantly setting new challenges for myself.

Girl, 14, Australia

No, I never get bored in school. I always have something to do. Even if I don't have work to do, I talk to my friends, who make my days fun. I don't think I'll ever get bored.

Girl, 14, Texas

I am ALWAYS bored in school. I have to fight to keep myself from zoning out and letting my boredom reach into other areas of my life. Mostly, what I do is draw or think about what's going on in my life. I think about what I'm going to do when I get home, poems or stories I want to write, conversations I've had, etc. It doesn't help much.

Girl, 14, Illinois

Yes. In one class, the teacher repeats the same information in answer to questions from classmates who don't bother to listen the first time. I think he should arrange to repeat himself after class, not during.

Boy, 15, North Carolina

"No, I never get bored in school. I always have something to do."

I can see through teachers' attempts to just make us busy or fulfill state requirements or try to make us do better on standardized tests.

Girl, 15, Minnesota

I get bored when I am sitting near the back of the room. It makes it difficult to keep my mind on the subject when I am so far away from it.

Boy, 15, Ohio

I read or doodle when I get bored. I used to talk, but that got me into trouble.

Girl, 16, Kansas

I often find myself bored in school, mainly in American History. To relieve the boredom, I either stare into the blank faces of my classmates or act out inappropriately. I don't believe this is what I should be doing, but my boredom often gets the best of me.

Boy, 16, Iowa

School becomes boring when a teacher is explaining something trivial to someone who was just too lazy to take notes or read the material. I used to read in class when I got bored, but no more—that offends teachers.

Boy, 17, Nebraska

What gets me bored? Ignorance in the general population.

Boy, 17, Georgia

When I'm bored, I usually daydream. That way, my subconscious can partially pick up what the teacher is saying and, if I find it interesting, I can tune back in.

Girl, 17, Indiana

When I get bored:
1. When there is no definite goal or objective to follow.
2. When there is not a real reason for doing something.
3. When the work seems designed for a baby and not someone who wants to go to an Ivy League or other prestigious college.

Girl, 17, Wisconsin

## Reflection Connection

Gifted students often name boredom as a reason they don't like school. However, boredom is only a symptom. If you want to relieve boredom, you have to find the real problem—the **cause** of your boredom. Just saying "I'm bored" to a teacher is unlikely to get any noticeable change in your assignments. If you're bored at school, figure out the specific reasons. Is it simply that the work is too easy? Is it that subjects don't seem connected to the "real world"? Once you know the reasons, analyze them and try to think of specific ways to change them. What specifically can you ask teachers to do that might help make school more engaging?

## What activities do teachers do that make learning worthwhile?

A really fun activity that makes learning worthwhile is having a contest with teams to see who can find the answer the fastest.
Girl, 13, Texas

Whatever the activities, I think public schools need to group classes by ability and not by age.
Boy, 13, Massachusetts

In home ec, we actually sew and cook.
Boy, 13, Iowa

They ask students questions. They debate. They make students use their brains instead of just reciting information. They ask students to think, to imagine, to become.
Girl, 14, England

My gifted teacher makes things more interesting by assigning fun homework. For one book report, we made airplanes, and for another, we built a covered wagon. My science teacher allows us to do experiments but, unfortunately, he hasn't let us blow anything up yet.
Boy, 14, Kentucky

Most teaching is done in a "one size fits all" approach and gifted kids are not "normal" size. There need to be teachers who teach YOU, not THE CLASS.
Girl, 14, Ohio

I like it best when I can choose my own topics to study and then the teacher builds the school stuff I do around that.
Girl, 14, Colorado

As long as teachers do things differently a little bit each day, I feel like I'm learning something.
Boy, 14, Ohio

Our gifted class is very different from our other classes, not so much because of what the teacher does, but because the students in it really do care about learning.
Boy, 14, Australia

Teachers try to make learning fun, but most of the time, the students don't see what they do as enjoyable. Most of the students don't believe that school or learning can be fun or worthwhile.
Girl, 15, Wisconsin

"My science teacher allows us to do experiments but, unfortunately, he hasn't let us blow anything up yet."

I think the American public school system tries to get everyone to the same level (which, sadly, means ignoring those who are ahead) and tries to improve students' weak points. This is demotivating for everyone. Why not let kids learn what they are interested in? Offer choices . . . and then set graduation requirements.

Girl, 15, Massachusetts

In my gifted program, we take Media Production classes. We write, produce, film, and edit individual and small-group films. Since there is a possibility that I may have a job in media in the future and we are surrounded by media every day, it makes sense to me. It's also a lot of fun.

Boy, 15, Washington

When teachers make things more fun than they usually are, class is great. I've had some teachers who just write things that we have to copy down, and that is so boring. Then I've had others that show us how what we are learning can relate to ourselves and our world. THOSE are the teachers I remember.

Girl, 14, Connecticut

I think that having the students be actively involved is the most important thing teachers can do. Many teachers are boring because they don't care about the subject themselves, or they can't make the kids care, so the kids act up and the teachers blame us. In specific terms, I guess that intelligent class discussions, out-of-class reading, and no pointless worksheets designed for testability make for an exciting education.

Girl, 14, Illinois

A teacher who is really interested in what he or she teaches is so much easier to listen to than one who is following some schedule just to make me do well on tests. I get excited when a teacher not only doesn't mind answering my questions, but is able to answer them comprehensively.

Boy, 15, North Carolina

Some of my teachers tell stories in class to liven it up. My social studies teacher does this and, occasionally, he lets us take a little break so as to break up the boredom of routine.

Boy, 15, Texas

The only time school is fun is when people speak up in debates.

Girl, 16, Oklahoma

I really like classroom discussion. It gives kids a chance to think and possibly correct the teacher.

Boy, 16, Pennsylvania

In middle school, where I was the happiest, I tested out of history and English. I was allowed to choose special projects. First, I wrote and directed a film on the French Resistance in World War II, engaging twenty-seven classmates in the production. Also, I did a Civil War project and displayed memorabilia. I had a great leadership teacher who helped me understand that I was valuable and he kept me soooooo busy by having me organize the Special Olympics for my school. When I was in his classes, it felt like home.

Boy, 16, California

It's not really an activity, but teachers need to learn how to understand and be there to listen to your problems.

Girl, 17, Australia

# In Their Words: Sarah, Age 19

Too often, young adults are racked with regrets for not having taken full advantage of the opportunities offered to them. But for me, high school graduation was more like standing at the pinnacle of a mountain I had long been climbing. I was exhausted from my journey, but greatly satisfied with the view, eager to begin the next leg of my trek.

But that's getting ahead of myself. Let me start when I was younger. My hometown is a middle-class suburb of Cleveland, Ohio. My family is as average as they come: a mom, a dad, a younger sister and brother, two cats, and a dog. My mom was an emergency room nurse but is now getting a degree to become a teacher (a random career switch that I will never understand), and my dad is a firefighter who also owns his own business.

My hobbies are many, mostly involving music. I play trumpet and piano and I sang in my high school choir and danced in the show choir. Academically, I've been in a gifted program since fourth grade. That program eventually morphed into AP and honors classes in high school, and if an honors course was available, I took it. I'm not a philosopher, a superhero, or Miss America—just a human being who happens to be gifted. Socially, I'm still a teenage girl who hangs out with friends, watches movies, and plays video games. My boyfriend is an airman in the U.S. Air Force, currently stationed in England. I see him rarely but think about him always.

My life during school—and my life to this day—has always been a draining and exhilarating blur of music rehearsals, challenging classes, unwavering straight A's, volunteering, working part-time, late nights, long days, and little sleep. My life is a balancing act and it is a dance: complex, vigorous, continuous, orchestrated, random, and always in motion. And no matter how much I may try to "take it easy," my soul seems to know no other way of life than this.

When I consider what types of educational experiences helped me to become so focused and passionate, I reflect on the many

→

exceptional teachers I have had. Among my teachers was Dr. D., who took our "Project Plus" seventh- and eighth-graders on monthly fieldtrips to various places to open up our minds and hearts, teaching us things that can't be learned within the confines of a classroom. We've been to such diverse places as Cleveland's West Side Market, where the culture of Cleveland's past collides with the cuisine of too many nations to remember. We went to Lakeview Cemetery, where history and art come together in a 290-acre resting place for such luminaries as President James Garfield, "Untouchable" Eliot Ness, and billionaire John D. Rockefeller. We explored a burn center and neonatal intensive care unit at a children's hospital. I recall thinking that the kids we saw with severe burns were so like me, but their wounds forbade them from appreciating all of the wonders and joys childhood offers.

Even when we didn't go on a trip (although one of Dr. D's favorite lines was, "if it's free and interesting, we'll go there!"), we still learned. We "heard" a lecture given in school by a deaf individual through an interpreter; we listened to poetry by Langston Hughes put to music by a local performer; we each "became" Edgar Allan Poe as we created and then recited "poe"etry and prose dressed in a long black robe and a top hat. In doing these activities and going to the places we did, one of life's biggest doors was opened for me: *reality*. In fact, following our hospital visit, our class sponsored a fundraiser called "Coffee for a Cause," where kids in grades 7 through 12 shared literary and musical pieces at the public library for our audience while donated baked goods and coffee were sold. It has since become a tradition, and in the seven years that "Coffee for a Cause" has existed, more than $9,500 has been raised for the burn center's children. I wrote about this project at Dr. D's urging, and it was accepted for

"When I consider what types of educational experiences helped me to become so focused and passionate, I reflect on the many exceptional teachers I have had."

publication in a national magazine, as the centerpiece article. As an eighth grader (which is what grade I was in when I wrote the piece) I felt honored to see my name in print yet humbled to know the source of that honor was children whose lives were touched by tragedy. Throughout the two years of Project Plus, my classmates and I learned about the world, ourselves, and each other.

Later, some Project Plus alumni (we were now in high school) accompanied Dr. D. to the United States Holocaust Memorial Museum in Washington, D.C. The trip was made financially feasible thanks to a grant from the local chapter of the Anti-Defamation League (ADL). It was by far the most meaningful trip I have ever taken. I was deeply moved by the images and artifacts at the Museum. Walking through a boxcar that had deported thousands to concentration camps, viewing the barracks from Auschwitz, and listening to the voices of survivors broadened my understanding of the evil and ignorance mankind is capable of performing. I came away from this trip resolved to never again take any aspect of my life for granted, and vowed never to let the populace of the world commit such a crime against itself ever again.

Several months after our visit, Dr. D. was notified that the ADL could no longer fund these trips. However, a glimmer of hope remained: the ADL was holding its annual meeting and several individuals with the financial means to underwrite our trip would be there. Dr. D. asked me to represent the dozens of students who had gone on this trip, and I gladly accepted.

I had no idea what the experience would be like when I said "yes." I had never before seen the inside of a country club (which is where the meeting was being held) or been in the presence of people of such wealth and distinction. I was the only person younger than 35 and, in all conceivable ways, I felt perfectly out of place. When I was introduced, Dr. D. gave me a wink of "good luck" as I stepped to the podium. I was relieved to see smiling faces looking back at me. I introduced myself, delivered my partially preconceived/partially improvised speech about the impact of this trip on me, and then thanked everyone with as much eloquence and confidence as I could muster.

As I returned to my seat, I was utterly surprised to be showered with furious applause and pats on the back from perfect strangers. Shortly after the meeting, we were notified that we had gained

→

enough financial support to not only fund our program, but also to send several other high school groups from our region on this powerful trip to the Holocaust Memorial Museum. I felt incredibly contented to know that I was able to give back to a program that had given me so much.

Experiences like these visits to the children's hospital and the Holocaust Memorial Museum instill the importance of compassion, humility, and wisdom into teenagers like me. These are the qualities from which all good things originate.

As I move forward in my life, my plan is to earn a doctorate in pharmacy. I attend a program at Ohio State University that usually requires eight years to complete, but that I will complete earlier due to a special honors program to which I've been admitted. After graduation, I plan to enter the field of nuclear pharmacy, where I hope to make a significant contribution in the area of oncology (cancer), as it relates to pharmacology.

My goals are set; my goals are strong. Underlying them all is my desire to remember that compassion, humility, and wisdom are the truest gifts that I can return to humanity. That would make me proud, as well as my parents. My guess is that Dr. D. will approve too.

## Some schools have special programs and teachers for gifted students. Is this a good idea?

Gifted programs are a good idea because we need a place to feel safe from the torment and jeers from other students. We need a place where we can be, well, "gifted."

Girl, 13, Ohio

They are a good idea because they give us the opportunity to show our talents by doing different types of projects. They are a bad idea because some of these projects can cause the students to have more homework, which we sometimes can't handle.

Girl, 13, Texas

Gifted programs are not a good idea. It's like what the Nazis did. They put certain people in certain camps, judging them. When you do this, it gives other students a good reason to discriminate against gifted kids, to make fun of us.

Boy, 14, Texas

I think it is good to have some special classes, but not all of them. Math and science are the only courses that should be gifted ones because they are the subjects you need most in life. I have had gifted classes in every subject and it is too hard with everyone breathing down your neck.

Boy, 14, California

They should never think about removing these programs because they are very good for gifted kids. Without them, smart kids might lose their potential which would be catastrophic to their futures.

Boy, 14, Texas

If you separate gifted students from their friends who may not be gifted, that's just wrong. You could have one period where the gifted kids got together, but taking students from their friends is just wrong.

Boy, 14, Kentucky

I'm in a gifted class and I have met other kids who function at my level. But it also alienates us from the rest of the school. (Actually, I'm still bored in my gifted class, but at least now, when I roll my eyes, my friends understand why.)

Girl, 14, Ontario

Every school should have such a program. Gifted children don't often share the usual interests of their peers. By gathering together other children like them, they develop a better understanding of themselves and can express their gifts (as odd as they may be) to people like themselves.

Girl, 15, New Jersey

Yes, because gifted programs prevent students from getting bored in school. We do not perform as well as we could if we are not challenged.

Boy, 15, Arizona

Gifted classes were the only things that kept me sane in my early education. I think it's essential that public schools have gifted programs because not all families can afford to send their gifted kids to specialized schools. My gifted classes challenged me while allowing me to be creative and unique.

Girl, 15, Indiana

As with any program, there are advantages and disadvantages. For example, in my school, you are in the same gifted class for six years. We do become a close knit group, most of us, but some people don't quite fit in, so they spend six years with people who aren't as similar to them as they had hoped. Also, when we are together for so long—four years with one teacher and two with another—things start to get monotonous.

Boy, 15, Ohio

No, because I think most students are shut off from their peers in gifted classes, creating a gap with no bridge for the slower students to make friends with the gifted students. Also, if someone's IQ is one or two points below the cutoff but they still think at a high level, why shouldn't they be allowed in the gifted program?
Boy, 15, Indiana

"The classes need to challenge us, but they also need to offer a pretty relaxed atmosphere so we can actually have a little fun in school."

Gifted programs have enormous potential to help students develop and understand their abilities. Complete isolation, though, could be harmful, both in the sense of elitism and because it is important to understand that the majority of the population thinks a little differently than you do.
Girl, 15, Massachusetts

Yes, gifted programs should definitely be in schools, especially if the teacher understands gifted kids. The classes need to challenge us, but they also need to offer a pretty relaxed atmosphere so we can actually have a little fun in school.
Girl, 15, Tennessee

Although gifted programs are a good idea, they tend to set gifted students apart from the other kids, which incites jealousy and ill will.
Boy, 15, New York

I think gifted programs are a great idea IF the teachers in the programs know what they are doing. A lot of time, it's just, "Oh, these kids are gifted; they should be doing a lot more work." But it's all busywork! We need more interesting things to do and people who understand us.
Girl, 15, Illinois

I shudder to think what it would be like if gifted classes were abolished! What really needs to happen is a common acceptance of radical acceleration—skipping multiple grades, if you can handle it. I'm glad that now that I'm in high school, the director of my magnet school encouraged me to test out of normal classes and get into AP calculus BC and AP chemistry in my sophomore year.

Girl, 15, Georgia

I have a kindred spirit, a boy my age who lives 600 miles from me whom I get to visit once a year for a week or so. He is as "terminally gifted" as I am and we are interested in the same things. If I could have had classes with kids like that, I think that is what heaven must be like.

Boy, 16, North Carolina

When gifted students are challenged, they usually try harder and achieve more. They also learn more things.

Girl, 16, New Mexico

I am opposed to any and all sorts of "tracking programs" and "elite schools" because they not only separate the child from his friends, they divide parents as well. Gifted programs or schools further divide the already cliquish youth cohort.

Girl, 17, New York

I never went to a school that had special teachers and programs for gifted students. We were just taken aside and given extra work, which we always resented, because it was just busywork. The alternative to busywork was that we helped out the really slow kids in class. That was slightly better, but being treated differently from everyone else made other kids resent us.

Girl, 19, North Carolina

## Reflection Connection

Special programs for gifted students have always been controversial, with some people seeing them as a necessary part of a school's operation, and others seeing them as elitist. Where do **you** stand on this issue? Should schools provide supplemental programs for gifted students? Also, project a few years ahead and consider if you would want your own child to participate in a gifted program. If so, why? If not, why not?

## If you're in a gifted program, how do you feel about it?

My favorite thing about our gifted program is that I know and like everyone in it. So, when the teacher tells us he is about to assign groups for a project, I can look around the room, and sure, there are some I would want to work with more than others, but there is no one I don't want to work with.

Girl, 13, Florida

I love having a gifted program because you make such great relationships with your peers and you can work at a faster pace without other kids to slow you down.

Boy, 13, New Jersey

I love it and I look forward to it every week. I always get to do something different. I know some kids say, "It's not fair; why can't I go?" or "Are you going to that smart kids class again?" but I feel that if these kids applied themselves they could probably be exposed to the same benefits that I've enjoyed.

Girl, 13, Pennsylvania

I liked the experience but I had my schedule changed to regular classes because the stress was causing me to have migraines, and those migraines made me miss school at least once each week.

Boy, 14, Texas

Three times a week, instead of being bored in class, "learning" what we learned three years ago, I have an opportunity to creatively solve future problems in society, discover science much deeper than we ever do in class, and live history in the form of skits and other creative ways.

Girl, 14, New Jersey

I love it! It is like a home in school for me. People understand me there.

Boy, 14, New Jersey

Mr. P. is a wonderful GT teacher. We have a schedule for some things, but if a kid has an idea he would like to investigate, Mr. P. usually says okay. We also get ten minutes or so at the end of class to test out any new toys of his.

Girl, 14, Texas

I went through elementary school in a gifted class and I got to know my classmates better than I know my own sister.

Girl, 14, New Jersey

My gifted program is a great way to get to meet some worthwhile friends.

Boy, 14, Nebraska

I know for a fact that our school gets extra money for having us in this GT class. I have no problem with being gifted, but the class is just a bunch of extra work for no good reason. The administration forces us into this class so the school can make an easy buck. *They* should take this class and see how they feel!

Girl, 14, Texas

The program is very cool because we get to experience much different stuff. Our teacher is very strict and she doesn't make any exceptions or accept any late work. She is playing the role of our boss and she's making us turn in our work each day. Also, I'm very glad to be in this program because people don't make fun of my being smart.

Boy, 14, Texas

I do not like my program because it is too much hard work. They push us a lot harder than they do other students in normal classes. I don't even know how I got into this program. I don't think I'm gifted at all.
Boy, 14, Texas

I am now in all accelerated classes in high school and they are a disappointment. They're supposed to prepare us for the ACT instead of teaching us anything interesting.
Girl, 15, Illinois

Honors classes are ideal. The students are generally mature, attentive, and passionate about their ideas. The teacher can spend time teaching the significance of the subject to interested pupils instead of spewing facts to a dormant audience in the blind hope that they won't fail the next test. The classroom "society" is accepting and friendly. Therein lies the true incentive to learn.
Girl, 15, Wisconsin

Sometimes it helps you and your future, because you can finish your classes earlier and instead of taking pre-algebra in eighth grade you take it sooner. But at the same time, you feel stressed and depressed sometimes—you even want to cry. Everybody you know expects a lot when you're in a gifted class. Every minute of your life becomes harder for you.
Boy, 15, Texas

I've learned that teachers do not want a profoundly gifted kid in their class—they told me so directly. They had no idea where I should be, but they didn't want me with them.
Boy, 16, Iowa

I was in a gifted program in elementary school, but it wasn't very successful. Still, I felt relieved that at least someone was trying to challenge us. If our program would have had the support of the school, it might have taken off, but that was not the case.
Girl, 16, Michigan

The current program I'm in is great, because the structure is essentially nonexistent. The biggest advantage is that there are virtually no restrictions imposed, whether learning related or not. A good many people spend a lot of time doing homework or talking and our "teacher" (more of a "guide") doesn't mind, as long as we eventually produce something (keyword: "eventually")!

Boy, 16, Iowa

My gifted programs were great because they gave me a place to vent.

Girl, 16, Minnesota

I once attended an elite high school. The folks were generally nice, but underneath the preppy exteriors was the most cutthroat bunch you'll ever meet. Going back to my "ghetto school" was a breath of fresh air.

Boy, 17, Pennsylvania

Our gifted program, Spectrum, begins in elementary school and offers classes that are filled with the creativity that other classes lack. In high school, the program shifts, and a select group of guidance counselors works to prepare the students for college. All the way through their tenure in Spectrum, gifted students are taken on cultural field trips and other places to expand their minds.

Boy, 18, Tennessee

I didn't like my gifted programs all that much, but now I realize that I would have gone out of my mind with boredom if it hadn't been for the gifted program. That's not to say I wasn't bored, I usually was; it's just to say that I was less bored with the program than I would've been without it.

Girl, 19, Virginia

My school had gifted programs starting in fourth grade. This seemed to work well, as we received a portion of every day with gifted students, while we were essentially integrated with other students as well. The program was extremely rewarding, intellectually stimulating, and provided time for creativity and exploration. It also fostered close friendships with other gifted students.

Boy, 19, Massachusetts

## What makes a "gifted teacher"?

A gifted teacher is someone who enjoys teaching, who can get kids under control easily while still having fun, and who has ways to make the classroom "come alive" by their enthusiasm and knowledge.

Girl, 13, Maine

A gifted teacher can get you interested in anything, even if it's only a brick.

Boy, 13, Iowa

The teacher has to know the subject area and understand that she doesn't know everything. She must set a high standard for everybody and expect that everyone will reach that standard.

Girl, 13, New Jersey

"A gifted teacher can get you interested in anything, even if it's only a brick."

Gifted teachers are those who aren't intimidated by kids who are smarter than they are.

Girl, 13, Texas

They understand how stressed students can get at times because they have been there themselves.

Boy, 13, Maine

A gifted teacher is someone who is smart and understands the kids. It's hard to find teachers like these because most teachers just like to judge people. *All* teachers should be very good at what they do and if they aren't, they should be fired.

Boy, 13, Arizona

Gifted teachers aren't necessarily gifted in the same way a student might be. Their giftedness tends to be based more upon their style, as they are able to do these things: relate the subject matter to the students' lives; devise interesting areas for exploration; and create an atmosphere in the classroom where the students really want to be there. No subject, no matter how tempting to the student, remains interesting with a dull teacher.

Girl, 14, Australia

I think a gifted teacher should be able to relate to gifted children either by being gifted themselves or having their own gifted children.

Girl, 14, Ohio

Teachers who are hard working and go out of their way to make sure kids are learning are gifted teachers. They have to be very excited about what they are doing and they have to have a good attitude toward students.

Boy, 14, Texas

If they have the ability to tie things in and make them fun, while allowing leniency for random discussions that add to the class, and if they are able to get any student hooked on a subject, whatever it is, then they are gifted.

Boy, 14, Connecticut

A gifted teacher takes part in activities with students instead of just sitting back watching them do activities. Also, they will volunteer their time to help tutor you if you need it.

Boy, 14, Texas

I don't know. I've never had one.

Girl, 14, Ontario

A gifted teacher can know exactly what to say to make a student feel gifted, special, or even just better. I think it is amazing how many teachers at my school are like this.

Girl, 14, Ohio

I have had some really gifted teachers who can deal with difficult situations without losing their tempers or sending kids to the office. Those are gifted teachers to me.

Boy, 15, Minnesota

Teachers are gifted when they are able to learn every student's personality. Teachers also are gifted if they are able to teach a disabled child without taking away from the learning opportunities of the rest of the class.

Boy, 15, Ohio

There are many people who can be teachers, but only certain people in the world are gifted at teaching. These few just seem able to express themselves and what they are trying to teach more easily. I think of these teachers as the ones that you remember when you get older. Not only do they teach you school lessons, they teach you life lessons.

Girl, 15, Oklahoma

When teachers know what the heck they are talking about rather than just reading from the textbook, that is a gifted teacher.

Boy, 15, Massachusetts

A gifted teacher has the ability to reach out to any kind of student, whether it is a struggling student or one who is super-intelligent. Just like a student is supposed to listen and try to understand what the teacher says, the opposite should be true as well.

Girl, 15, Texas

Being able to talk one-on-one with a student as well as to the whole class makes a teacher gifted. I have a teacher I would tell almost anything and I know she wouldn't tell if I asked her not to. If a student has confidence in their teacher, that is a MAJOR plus.

Boy, 16, Pennsylvania

A gifted teacher is someone who engages everyone. I have one teacher who makes statements and then calls on a random student to state their opinion on that statement. Then he leaves the floor open to anyone who wants to challenge and/or agree with the student.

Girl, 16, Ohio

I have a shining example of a gifted teacher. In third grade, instead of assigning research on one of an approved list of barnyard animals, Ms. S. asked me to come up with a topic I would like to study. I got to spend over a month reading books on quantum physics. Wow! I will never forget Ms. S.!

Boy, 16, North Carolina

The ability to control our eccentricities.

Boy, 17, Washington

"When I was 10 years old, I took AP calculus BC. On the first exam, I answered all ten questions in about ten minutes. When I turned in my test with the ten answers (which were all correct), Mr. F. asked me, 'Where's your work?' I asked, 'What work?'

"Instead of telling me that I had done it wrong, Mr. F. talked with me for a while. He started by saying that the way I did it was a wonderful talent. He really tried to understand how I approached the math—that when I see a problem, I also see the answer. I had no clue that other people took little steps to get from the question to the answer. Instead of just telling me I was wrong, Mr. F. explained that it was important for me to learn what steps other people take because someday I may have a new concept in math, and so I would need to be able to speak the language to explain it to other mathematicians. Also, he said that even I would eventually get to a level of math where I had to take some steps.

"Mr. F. spent a lot of extra time that semester helping me to understand about taking steps. And because he explained the need so thoroughly, I didn't feel that he was trying to make me slow down or to do it 'his' way for no good reason. It was hard to learn what steps other people take, but over the next few years I found out just how indispensable it is to understand about taking steps."

Boy, 15, North Carolina

## Reflection Connection

Imagine you have been asked to serve on a local school committee to select a teacher for a newly formed gifted program. Part of your job is to generate a list of characteristics and skills that you hope the successful candidate will possess. What personal and professional qualities would you like to see in hiring this teacher for your school district's gifted program? Why did you choose the attributes that you did?

## How could school be improved?

Honestly, I have so much frustration in school that I find it hard to come up with suggestions. I suppose the only way is to create a classroom for the top ten or so children in each grade. Otherwise, the best thing to do is to find another learning environment where you can meet other students like yourself and meet teachers who understand you and respect your ability to learn.

Boy, 13, New York

I think school people need to remind students that just because they are not in gifted programs does not mean that they are not smart.

Girl, 13, Texas

Teachers could give us different spelling words. I mean, would it kill them to come up with more challenging words than "stocky" and "diagram"? Those are just a little too easy.

Girl, 13, Ohio

Teachers should try to learn with us instead of always trying to teach us. And, they can't be afraid to have a student who is smarter than they are.

Girl, 13, Colorado

Every child has different learning needs, and teachers should try to determine what those needs are.

Boy, 14, Colorado

Instead of focusing on making students sit still and passively absorb information that doesn't interest them just so they can pass tests, teachers can try to get students to actively participate. Most of all, I NEVER want to hear a teacher say (and I have often heard this), "Oh, you don't need to learn that because it is not on the test."

Girl, 14, Illinois

In elementary school I would always get very excited when I spent a day with people like me. There are special education programs for students who learn slower than others and I think there is no excuse for not having a similar program for gifted students.

Boy, 14, Ohio

I love being challenged, but sometimes, I just want a break, which I can't have. Last Wednesday was the first time I can remember in two years when I had no homework due the next day.

Girl, 14, Washington

My school doesn't do anything extra for gifted students, so I am always bored by teachers explaining the area of rectangles. I think in eighth grade I ought to be past that by now!

Boy, 14, Oklahoma

Teachers could have us get to know other students like ourselves more so that we can have people to relate to. I mean, we should still be able to hang out with other kids, but I don't feel that I know many other gifted people.

Girl, 14, Maine

Less review and more assignments that actually involve thinking.

Girl, 14, England

Teachers could better enforce rules against bullying.

Boy, 14, Massachusetts

"Let me move at my own pace. Don't find me busywork to do while everyone else catches up. Don't expect me to go slower to stay with the group."

Teachers could definitely stop teaching everything the textbook way. Instead of reading about history, go see it relived, things like that. Those are the types of things you remember and that really make you understand what you are learning.

Girl, 15, Connecticut

Let me choose at least one area of interest for me to study. Let me choose what books to read. Let me move at my own pace. Don't find me busywork to do while everyone else catches up. Don't expect me to go slower to stay with the group.

Boy, 15, North Carolina

Teachers could like their jobs enough to make us want to like ours.

Boy, 15, Nebraska

Give me the work, theory, idea, and then let me run with it and figure it out for myself.

Girl, 15, Iowa

Let's add some humor to classrooms. In my gifted program, we are always laughing, cracking stupid jokes, and doing stupid things. It's wonderful.

Girl, 15, Oregon

Don't give kids the idea that it is okay to be mediocre. Make each class applicable.

Girl, 16, Illinois

I would get rid of kids who don't want to be in school and don't want to learn. They make it harder for the rest of the kids to learn.

Boy, 16, Pennsylvania

Forget grade levels. Don't try to force your concept of socialization on me. If you put me with other students who are basically kind and at my academic level, I will appear to you to be a properly "socialized" kid. If you put me with bullies or kids with lower abilities, I will appear to avoid contact with my classmates and you will put labels on me that are unfair.

Boy, 16, North Carolina

I would like to see more schools exclusively for gifted students; schools that employ only teachers who are committed to their jobs and treat students like responsible people. I would make these schools accessible to low income families, like mine.

Girl, 16, Indiana

Teachers could stick up for us, give us more challenging work, don't pick us out of the crowd in class, but do things with us discreetly.

Girl, 16, Wisconsin

I would suggest putting us in smaller classes so we could learn at our own rate. Also, get rid of those time-consuming standardized tests.

Boy, 17, Michigan

# Reflection Connection

Many gifted students have felt "uncool," left out, or picked on at one time or another due to their giftedness. While some kids ignore it when people judge them this way, others respond by downplaying or disguising their abilities. Have you ever felt excluded or ridiculed because you're gifted? If so, how did you (or do you) react? If you haven't, how do you think you would react if you did? What do you think school officials can do to make schools a "safe" place to be smart?

## What will school be like until graduation?

I'd rather not know. I like to take things day-by-day.

Boy, 13, New York

I expect school to get more and more challenging as I go along. Because I am already in advanced classes, I expect to get further and further ahead of students in regular education. I'm already taking algebra a year earlier than I am supposed to.

Boy, 13, Texas

I think that school will be the same as it has been since kindergarten—easy. I will just have to suck it up and stick through all the boring stuff.

Girl, 13, Maine

"I hope that it will be pleasingly difficult—neither too hard nor too easy."

School will come easily because I remember information better than most students my age. I will keep up my good grades and continue to work hard because I am determined to go to college (although I don't know how I'll pay for it) and then get a good-paying job doing something I love.

Boy, 14, Ohio

If I survive, I will have taken one of two paths: I will have either become a neurotic overachiever, becoming valedictorian or salutatorian, or I will have chosen creativity and personal fulfillment and have an A or A- average. Knowing me, I will probably pick the second.

Girl, 14, Illinois

It will continue to be uncertain. I never know what is going to happen next, what opportunities will open for me, what I will be able to do or not do. Exams will be uncertain. Achievement will be uncertain. Grades will be uncertain. Everything will be in constant flux, and I like it that way.

Girl, 14, Australia

When I move to a residential gifted school this fall, I will, for the first time, be in an academically rigorous environment, and I can't wait. If I can stick it out there, high school will be challenging and exciting—I'll move on to college with ease.

Girl, 15, Indiana

Boring and repetitive, at least until they allow me to take AP courses. I wish they would let me now, as a sophomore. Until then, I'll keep myself occupied with my extracurriculars.

Boy, 15, Iowa

I hope that it will be pleasingly difficult—neither too hard nor too easy.

Boy, 16, Wisconsin

# Family Life: Being Gifted at Home

**E**veryone has at least one, some have several, and each one is different. We're referring, of course, to families. Before school ever begins, you gain much of what you know from the home front. Your family can be your greatest source of support, encouragement, and memories.

Of course, families also can be a source of misunderstandings, hurt feelings, and endless annoyances. And families with gifted kids can experience challenges that other families do not. For example, if a mother of a gifted kid is told from the time he's a toddler that "your son is so smart!" then that mom might ratchet up her expectations for this child without even knowing it. Or, if a dad is so proud that his daughter comes in first in everything she does, he may brag about her exploits to visitors, friends, and cousins—without thinking about how his daughter feels about that bragging. Also, sibling comparisons can be an issue in families with gifted kids, especially if more than one child in the family is gifted. Competition—healthy or otherwise—occurs more often than it doesn't. All these factors can affect a gifted teen's development.

## What has your family said to you about being gifted? What are their expectations of you?

My parents expect me to do well and to study hard. I think my mother is scared of the genius stereotype.

Girl, 13, Massachusetts

They think that I have the talent to become something in my life that will be above the rest.

Boy, 13, Ohio

When they found out I was gifted, my parents said, "Do you really want to be in this program? You don't have to if you don't want to. It will be okay with us if you would rather not be in SPF or FPS or whatever it is called."

Boy, 13, Michigan

My parents do not believe that I am gifted, merely that I am somewhat bright. I refute this notion. I consider myself to be gifted and I work as such to gain the deserved recognition.

Girl, 14, Australia

My mom has always been proud of me and she compliments me whenever she can. As for my dad, when he was alive he was a great father. He didn't expect much from me, but I was always his "very good girl."

Girl, 14, Texas

My mom never tells me her expectations because she knows that I already understand them.

Boy, 14, Connecticut

They have said that they are very proud of me and they expect me to be the best in everything I do.

Girl, 14, Ohio

Because of my giftedness, my parents have said a great deal to me. They say that I must be a role model for students in lower grades. They also dictate that because I am gifted I must strive for a better and harder education than the normal curriculum offers. I feel that being a role model can add pressure to a mind that has already been compressed with a load of very hard and long work due to a very strict, high-level curriculum.

Boy, 14, Texas

Even though I am smart, it is hard to keep up with the standards my parents set for me. They tell me that I am smart, yet I am still struggling to keep my grades up.

Boy, 14, Oklahoma

Every time I do something wrong, my parents remind me that I am gifted. My parents forget the fact that being gifted also means being creative. I only wish that was the characteristic my parents would see in me the most.

Girl, 14, Missouri

My parents are always talking about me being gifted and how different I am compared to other people my age. They tell me how lucky I am to be smart and that I should never be ashamed of myself or anything I do. They expect my grades to be in the 90s, and they also expect me to do the right thing when I go to places like parties or movies.

Boy, 14, Texas

My parents say that being gifted will get me far in life and that I have to appreciate it. They don't think of me as a child but as an adult who is just smaller than they are.

Boy, 14, California

Because of my abilities, my parents expect me to be very responsible and to always keep my grades high. I sometimes feel they have asked me to grow up faster than normal. I just wish they wouldn't have such high expectations for my future. They tell me they just want me to be happy, but at the same time feel that is only possible by engaging in high-paying, high-prestige careers.

Girl, 15, Iowa

Since I am a gifted child, my parents said that I should compete with myself to be the best that I can be. They also said not to worry about the others. They expect me to get good grades, but an occasional C is okay with them. They certainly don't want me to get any zeroes—they told me that as soon as they were told I was gifted.

Boy, 15, Arizona

I sometimes think my mom is sick of my good grades. Sometimes I catch her saying, "Can't you just make a C once in a while?" (I don't even know if I could if I tried.)

Girl, 15, Indiana

When I was little, like 2 or 3 years old, they always told me that everyone has gifts—maybe being a good listener or running fast or whatever—and that my gifts were being good at reading and math. I also knew I was good at making babies happy, and I liked doing that, so I include that as one of my gifts.

Boy, 16, North Carolina

My parents always tell me that I can do better (like I haven't heard this enough!). They also expect me to have common sense and to use it, forgetting that I am a teenager and that teenagers do stupid stuff.

Girl, 16, Pennsylvania

My parents go on and on about how I should make a 98–100 percent in every class, graduate as valedictorian, go to West Point, serve in the military, and get a really high-paying job. It drives me crazy because, yes, I want to do those things, but not to the extent that they want me to. They don't see me getting married and having children. They see me in a huge house, probably by myself, with enough money to support them when they get old.

Girl, 16, Georgia

My parents haven't really said anything to me about being gifted, though I wish they would. I don't think my father is gifted, so I guess I can understand why he wouldn't be very comfortable talking about giftedness with me, but my mother is gifted, and I wish she would talk about it more often. I always felt out-of-step emotionally and intellectually with my classmates (even those in the gifted program) and I never knew why. I researched giftedness on my own and was surprised (and relieved) to find that my feeling of being different was related to my giftedness. I never knew how much being gifted colored a person's entire self. No one ever explained to me that a lot of my social/emotional difficulties and peculiarities came from being smart.

Girl, 17, New Jersey

"My parents say that being gifted will get me far in life and that I have to appreciate it."

My parents merely say that God granted me a gift and to not let it go to waste. They don't really expect anything of me, for they "know" I will go on to be successful in life.

Boy, 18, Tennessee

My parents don't talk to me unless I'm in trouble.

Boy, 18, Alabama

## Reflection Connection

Are the expectations your family has for you reasonable? Make a list of two to four expectations you feel your family has for you and rate each one from 1 (totally reasonable, easy to fulfill) to 5 (totally unreasonable, impossible to fulfill). Are their academic expectations of you higher or lower than their expectations in other areas, like social responsibility or emotional maturity? When (okay—if) you become a parent, how will your expectations for your own kids be similar to or different from those that your parents hold for you? Why?

# In Their Words: Azucena, Age 14

**M**y childhood was not easy. I was born in Chihuahua, Mexico, and before I was old enough for school I stayed home with my grandmother. My mother worked as a bank officer until late at night and my father worked as a car salesman. At 5 years old, I attended public school (in Mexico, you have three years in kindergarten/first grade). I had a happy life, but then everything turned horrible when my parents decided to divorce.

After the divorce I went to many different schools as my mother kept moving to find a better house. The schools used to cancel class often when it rained or snowed because the buildings were in such bad condition. Sometimes the rain leaked into the classrooms. I don't know if it is still as bad in Chihuahua, because my mom and I ended up moving to Colorado when I was 8 years old, and I've attended school here ever since.

To make the move, my mom had to sacrifice everything that she had worked for in Mexico: her car, her house, her career. She doesn't talk about these sacrifices, and I was really too young when we moved to recognize all that she was doing to make a better life for me. I am thankful for my mom's sacrifice, because I now have many friends and I am now bilingual. Speaking two languages will help me in my future, because I will be able to become a better doctor, which is my career goal. It is important for good doctors in Mexico to communicate with good doctors in America—I'll be able to do that.

My mom chose to come to Colorado because her aunt lived here and offered to let us stay in her house while she got a job and our own apartment. My mom is less stressed here, because in Mexico she had to work the whole day, coming home very late at night, to gain money for a living. Now, she works only until 6 p.m. and she earns the same money. Sometimes we even have some leftover money to go shopping and enjoy ourselves.

At the beginning, everything sounded interesting. Who wouldn't want to live in a place where tourists go to ski and snowboard and where everything seems better than where you lived before? I used to talk to my dad every day on the phone, which made me feel that we weren't so far apart. But now, we talk only once a week or so, and I get really sad when we hang up the phone. My stepdad is nice, but it's not the same as if I had my dad with me. I brought my dog from Mexico and that helped me to not feel so lonely. But my mom had to sell her when we moved to an apartment that didn't allow dogs. Can you believe it? She sold her for fifty dollars. Something you love doesn't have a price.

I realized I was gifted after I came to Colorado, even though no one had ever said anything about it in Mexico. I didn't know any English, and although I did not understand anything the teachers said, I looked at what we were doing and tried to understand it by myself. No matter how hard something seems, I think if I put enough effort into it, I can accomplish it. In the middle of second grade, my teacher gave my mom a letter explaining that

I could skip a grade. Unfortunately, my mom didn't want me to because she wanted me to go to school with kids my own age.

In seventh grade, my middle school principal gave me the opportunity to take the SAT. When I got to the testing center, I was very scared and didn't talk to anyone. All the other students there were already in high school. The only thing the teacher said was, "You are a valiant kid." Two months later, the results arrived. I didn't do well, but I didn't do so badly, either. Anyway, I'm really happy that I had the courage to take the SAT. It showed me what would be expected of me in high school. I now know what I have to do and learn to be ready . . . and I'm no longer scared. I know that my peers are going to be all nervous when they take the SAT for the first time, but I have already had my eyes opened to what this test entails.

In middle school, someone who studies is considered a nerd. Some consider it a good thing to be a nerd, but for others (like me), it is horrible. Most of the people who actually call me names are kids who share my Mexican heritage and they tease me in both English and Spanish. When they tease me, I try to show them that being smart is something I'm proud of (even though it makes me uncomfortable to say that). I joke with them and say, "Well, I might be a nerd, but I'm not the one who's going to have to spend my career selling fast food." They just laugh.

I could stop paying attention in class and get lower grades in order to fit in, but I won't do that. I made the decision to be who I am because my mom has always worked really hard to provide for me. How can I disappoint her? Still, it has been tough being the person I am because I'm always being bullied at school for being a gifted child.

I am really looking forward to turning 15, the year of my "quinceañera," a rite of passage in Mexico for young women. Young girls in Mexico start to think about quinceañera way ahead of time, wondering where the event will be held and what dress they will wear. At first I didn't want to do it, because a big part of quinceañera is dancing with your dad. But my mom has convinced me that it will still be a great event, no matter who I dance with.

Despite the many challenges I've had in my life, if I could change anything, I probably would not do so. Life occurs how it is meant to occur. If we all had the same happy life, it would be very, very boring.

## Do adults in your family ever brag about you or compare you to others? If so, how do you feel about this?

I sometimes find my parents comparing me to my brother, who is also gifted. I do like to hear the compliments, but I don't like the comparison because we are two different people and I sometimes feel that I need to live up to his standards.

Boy, 13, Michigan

I guess that's what parents are supposed to do. They like to have something to brag about. I feel like that is the only reason children are made in the first place, so that parents have something to brag about.

Boy, 13, Nebraska

One day I found out that I had gotten first place in the math competition and had gotten a trophy. That day, when I got home, my mom went straight to the phone, dialing the first number that came to her head. She then called every relative we have, including those in Dallas and Mexico. She did this for a whole day. Talk about embarrassment!

Girl, 13, Texas

My parents brag about my good grades all the time. My mom makes sure that everyone she works with knows about my awesome intelligence.

Boy, 13, Texas

Oh my gosh! My mom is always bragging! Every chance she gets! I hate it!

Boy, 13, Illinois

When I hear my parents (and sometimes even my sister) talking about me and making comments about my good grades, I feel embarrassed and I blush. But later, when I think about what it is that they were saying, I feel so good about myself that I want them to keep bragging about me!

Girl, 14, Kansas

These compliments that my parents make about me make me feel awesome! It feels like someone just gave me a birthday present or prize.
Boy, 14, Arizona

I've never caught my parents bragging about me but, if I did, I'd ignore them.
Boy, 14, Massachusetts

I have caught my parents talking about my abilities or comparing me to my sister. Sometimes, my sister overhears these conversations and she feels really, really bad, because she thinks she is not good enough. I hate when they do this because she is not old enough to be compared to my abilities.
Boy, 14, Arizona

No, they really don't brag about me. They make sure I know they are proud of me, but without exploiting me. My brothers were not as blessed as I in giftedness, but they have talents that I do not have, especially in thinking mechanically. In this way, we have all felt as equals and were very blessed to grow up in harmony with each other.
Girl, 15, Iowa

I feel that it is not fair that parents compare you to someone else and not to yourself. They don't understand that it is hard to match up to anyone else. They want you to become someone else that you are not.
Boy, 15, Colorado

"These compliments that my parents make about me make me feel awesome! It feels like someone just gave me a birthday present or prize."

I don't mean to sound conceited, but it would be nice if every once in a while I did hear my parents brag about me.

Girl, 15, Texas

I have heard my parents answer questions about me, which I guess could sound like bragging, but mostly, they are just being honest. (Boy, THAT sounds like bragging by me, doesn't it!)

Boy, 15, North Carolina

Sometimes I feel proud that they think so much of me, but other times I get tired of it and just want to be thought of as a regular person. I sometimes feel pressured to do exceptionally well in some things just to please my parents.

Boy, 15, California

Yes, they compliment me, which feels nice, although the compliments are unnecessary. I am other things besides smart.

Girl, 16, Pennsylvania

No, my parents never compare me to my brother, at least not in abilities. I'm very thankful for that because it would make me feel horrible or, when I was younger, it probably would have made me conceited.

Girl, 16, Indiana

I don't have brothers or sisters to be compared to, but I do catch my parents, especially my dad, bragging about me. It makes me feel kind of awkward, because I don't know how to react.

Boy, 16, New York

No one in my family is compared to anyone else—we're all in this thing together.

Girl, 16, Ontario

Compliments? No time for those. My parents regularly nag me about not working up to my capabilities.

Boy, 18, Kentucky

They don't really compare me to my sister because she has a learning disability and so that wouldn't really be fair. They have compared her grades to mine if she does better than I do. I think they do this to encourage her, but it still annoys me.

Girl, 19, Oklahoma

# Reflection Connection

How do you feel when parents or other family adults compliment you about something related to your giftedness? Do you feel differently if they compliment you privately or in front of your friends or siblings? And how about receiving compliments from friends or teachers—do you react to compliments from these people any differently than those you receive from your family?

## What has your family done to get you interested in new things? What haven't they discussed with you that you think they should?

There are college level biology, chemistry, and physics books lying around—and they are heavily used. In our home environment, everyone debates the validity of new medical research and everyone is expected to ask questions.

Girl, 13, New Jersey

My dad always talks about his job as a nuclear engineer since I find it interesting. I love to listen to him talk about anything because his voice is so quiet and soothing.

Girl, 14, Ohio

When I was little, they introduced me to sports and let me choose whatever sports that I wanted to go into. I liked that.

Boy, 14, Texas

I do feel, and I am quite embarrassed to say this, but I think they should talk to me about sex. I feel that could clear up a lot of my questions.

Boy, 14, Arizona

So far, my parents haven't done anything to get me interested in new topics. The only thing they do is tell me to study harder. I think they're afraid I will lose my GT title.

Girl, 14, Texas

I sit down with my mom and watch the news. She'll discuss things with me that I don't understand. (She explains things very well, in my opinion.)

Boy, 14, Connecticut

My parents pretty much leave me alone. Occasionally, my mom shows me old NOVA tapes to get me to learn about things they don't teach me in school.

Girl, 14, California

They really haven't done anything. All of my research and extended interests were of my own volition and motivation.

Boy, 15, Iowa

"Sometimes they insist on discussing matters I wish they'd avoid (homework and bedtimes), but that's about it."

I wish they would talk to me more about making friends, because I suck at this. At this point, I think I've missed out on the whole adolescent social thing.

Girl, 15, Indiana

My dad got me interested in computers when I was a baby by writing an alphabet program that had pictures of things I knew. "M" was a photo of my mom, "C" was a photo of dad's convertible, etc. I can't think of anything else except that we ALWAYS had lots of books around and I would choose whatever I wanted to read.

Boy, 15, North Carolina

I grew up in a Catholic family, but I wish they would have pursued religion more than they have. I want to go into depth with my religious study, but I hardly know where to begin. It just isn't enough for me to go to church on Sundays.

Girl, 16, Iowa

My parents really don't do anything to interest me in new topics, aside from clipping a newspaper article or getting me a book. However, they don't prohibit me from being interested in anything. (I'm not exactly sure how they *would* prohibit me, if they had the mind to do that.)

Girl, 16, Pennsylvania

My parents should discuss all the reasons I should have unlimited funds for video games (that's a joke). Honestly, I can't think of anything they should discuss but haven't. Sometimes they insist on discussing matters I wish they'd avoid (homework and bedtimes), but that's about it.

Boy, 16, North Carolina

My parents tried to introduce me to new things when I was younger, and I appreciate that. They should have introduced me earlier to theology and philosophy, but another relative helped me to discover more about those topics.

Boy, 17, Kansas

# In Their Words: Jason, Age 18

In some ways, I'm an anomaly. I've traveled the world due to my philanthropic work, yet I have never lived anywhere except in the same house in southern Indiana. As a National Merit Finalist, I had scholarships from many universities, yet I chose one (University of Evansville) right in my own backyard. I had the opportunity to take college courses when I was 14, yet I was homeschooled since age 10. I love to listen to Debussy and Mahler, yet two of my favorite bands are Siouxsie and the Banshees and Dir en grey. Yup, that's me! Just one anomaly after another.

Throughout my life, I've done a lot of what you might call "service projects." My first venture into this world of philanthropy came about due to the death of my grandmother–Nanny–when I was 9. Nanny and I had a very close relationship, since the whole family lived in the same house. Whenever I had a problem or felt unhappy, I would go to Nanny, who had a knack for making me feel better. She knew that I often felt odd at school and that I hated doing silly worksheets, but unlike my teachers and my worried parents, Nanny didn't remind me to do my homework or convey to me the feeling that I wasn't "doing my best." Nanny simply accepted me for who I was. Often, we "escaped" through the pages of books that she had given to me as gifts. Although these books were great presents, the best gift of all that Nanny gave me was allowing me to be myself and loving me for it.

After Nanny's death, my parents worried that I was depressed and, after talking to a psychologist (who has since become a great friend), we decided that the best way to honor Nanny's life was to celebrate it by helping others–something she had always done herself. Since we had loved to read together, I decided to begin a neighborhood newspaper, *The Informer,* and to donate the profits to the American Cancer Society, since Nanny had died of pancreatic cancer. Within a month, I could feel myself being lifted from the black hole that had engulfed me since Nanny's death.

Word of *The Informer* spread, and eventually my "neighborhood newspaper" grew to include subscribers in twenty-nine states and nineteen foreign countries! The focus of this newspaper was to highlight kids who were doing amazing things. Kids worldwide sent in articles, poetry, jokes, and drawings. By the time I stopped publishing *The Informer* when I began college, I had raised $7,000 for cancer research.

After I'd been publishing *The Informer* for about three months, a friend sent me a news story about a cellist in Sarajevo, Bosnia-Herzegovina, who had witnessed the massacre of twenty-two friends while they waited in a breadline. (Bosnia-Herzegovina was fighting a war for independence with Yugoslavia, and food was scarce.) The following day, dressed in the tuxedo he wore for his job with the Sarajevo Opera Orchestra, this cellist, Vedran Smailovic, went to the massacre site and played Albinoni's "Adagio in G Minor," which had been found in the ruins of Dresden, Germany, after Allied bombs fell there during World War II. Although surrounded by sniper fire, Smailovic kept his vigil for twenty-two days, one day to honor each one of his friends.

As I read this story, I saw the cellist's musical harmony as a symbol for social harmony and, even at age 10, I understood the only viable answer to war is social harmony. To honor Smailovic's courage, I founded The Cello Cries On, Inc., a not-for-profit organization whose mission is to unite and empower youth across cultural, racial, religious, and socioeconomic lines. A year later, when I was 12, I formed Youth for Peace, a delegation of international kids from fourteen countries who meet online to discuss issues of nonviolence and multiculturalism and to plan fundraising projects. Our first effort was to raise money to build a statue for Smailovic.

Then, at age 13, I designed a literacy program which involved a "book buddies" program at our library as well as a multicultural reading festival complete with native presenters, cultural videos, and all types of ethnic involvement. I also began a book drive to benefit family shelters and senior centers, collecting more than four thousand books.

Due to my work and the publicity it earned me from TV shows, magazines (I've been featured in *People, Teen People,* and *Time for Kids* magazines), and newspapers, I have had the opportunity to address school kids, youth groups, and educational and business audiences worldwide. I've been to the White House twice, and I have had the honor of meeting people like Hillary Clinton, Bill

Gates, and Oscar Arias, winner of the 1987 Nobel Peace Prize and president of Costa Rica.

Although I've had many supporters in my efforts, my work has not been without problems and obstacles. For example, when I first started *The Informer,* a few of my friends deserted and openly ridiculed me. The more my face showed up in the media, the more they taunted me. Still, I made a conscious decision that my work for cancer research was more important than a few bullies. But the pain I felt was real.

I called my parents "The Great Facilitators," because they were always at my side. For example, publishing *The Informer* required many skills that a 9-year-old doesn't have, so my dad helped me keep track of who had paid their subscriptions and who had not, and he also helped me to count money and figure costs and profit. However, my greatest obstacle to doing community service was simply a lack of mobility: 9-year-olds can't drive (not legally, anyway). Thus, my parents provided essential transportation—everywhere. For example, when I needed help from an attorney on how to form a not-for-profit corporation, my parents drove me several times to Indianapolis—a four-hour trip—to talk with various people. Every year during the week of my annual spring food drive, my parents would take me to talk to grocery store managers, hang up flyers around town, set up and retrieve collection boxes, and distribute the food door-to-door. They also provided transportation for the local youth group that I founded to get to the library's multicultural reading program I began. All this they did, and never asked for gas money!

These past nine years in philanthropy have been challenging, exciting, exhausting, and fun. Perhaps the most important lesson I've learned is that when you have suffered deep pain or tragedy, the best way to overcome those losses is to reach out to help someone else. As you reach out, you feel better about yourself. You grow confident; as your confidence peaks, you become empowered. And once empowered, you are able to empower others. You can make a difference in this world.

————>

As for my future, I plan to graduate with a double major in international studies and history. Later, I see myself as a musician or history professor, although thinking of a career right now is more than a bit scary.

As gifted teens, we are supposed to be becoming our own persons. Our ideas, passions, and interests will change, our tastes in music and literature will shift, and our political and religious views will probably vacillate. We will experiment—badly, at times—and make mistakes. But this is okay; in fact, it's more than okay. This is all just a part of the creative process that will continue throughout our lives.

## When are you happiest at home?

Love from my family is what makes me happiest. When I say "love," it means so many different things, such as just caring for me and supporting the things I do.

Boy, 13, Ohio

The Internet is a crucial, absolutely crucial, factor in my life. Being mentally connected through chatrooms, instant messages, message boards, and common fields of interest and similarities in personality is absolutely necessary to me.

Girl, 13, Australia

When I have really stressful days at school, I like to go home and just kick back. Even though that never happens, I try to imagine it like it did. I get so overwhelmed with having so much to do when school is done that being inactive makes me happiest at home (at least in theory).

Girl, 13, Texas

My cat is the only thing that makes me happy. She purrs when I pet her and is extremely playful. Since my brother is always mean and my parents are always busy, my cat is the only one who cheers me up.

Boy, 13, Texas

I love to be with my parents and my siblings. They are the best family I could ask for. At home they make me very happy, and they always buy me whatever I ask for.

Girl, 13, Texas

I love when my dad and I are doing everyday activities, like walking in the woods, watching TV, or just asking him a question I have about science or math. As a joke, we write on little strips of napkins or newspapers lots of equations to solve. I clearly remember when dad asked me to name ten ways to measure the height of a building with a barometer when I was 7. And just recently, we calculated vectors while watching *Fear Factor*.

Boy, 13, New Jersey

I'm happiest when I get some extra sleep—just to lie down and relax after a hard day.

Boy, 14, Maryland

My sister makes me happy because she is really silly and I need that. She is almost three years older than I am, but since I'm gifted, I can understand what she is talking about.

Girl, 14, Ohio

"If you are ever feeling down, bury your face in a cat's tummy as it purrs and see if you don't feel better!"

Just coming home to a nice clean house with no drama makes me happy. It makes me feel as if my household is peaceful even though I know we have problems, like any family.

Boy, 14, Iowa

My brother makes me very happy. It was a hard year of adjustment when my brother moved out to go to college. Suddenly, I didn't have my confidant anymore. I guess it was a good thing, though, because it forced me to make friends that I wouldn't have otherwise.

Boy, 15, Minnesota

All of my family makes me somewhat happy, except my stepdad. He does a lot of things I don't agree with, so I seldom even talk to him. Now my mom . . . that's a different story. There are times when we can be the best of friends and I feel I can tell her anything. She'll cheer me up when I am down or feeling lonely. But there are also times when we don't get along at all.

Girl, 15, Massachusetts

I feel guilty saying this, but my boyfriend makes me feel happiest when he is around. He is a college freshman and is not superbly intelligent, but since he is older, he is at my maturity level. He is my best friend. I feel like I can talk to him and he doesn't judge me for being young or smart. He makes me feel good about myself.

Girl, 15, Indiana

We have always had cats since I can remember. They are wonderful "purr"veyors of fuzz therapy. If you are ever feeling down, bury your face in a cat's tummy as it purrs and see if you don't feel better!

Boy, 15, North Carolina

At home, I like to do something I can do nowhere else: have time to myself. To relax, play with my pets, jump on the trampoline, or just listen to music.

Boy, 16, New York

What makes me happiest at home is music. Whenever I go home, I always listen to music, whether it is classical, hip-hop, or Mexican. For me, it creates another world that I just escape to. It can also inspire me when I do a project for school. Some of my best projects have come from that.

Boy, 16, Florida

I love to build model cars. This makes me satisfied with myself, especially when I finish a project. I also enjoy drawing, which brings out my innermost thoughts.

Girl, 16, Arizona

My music and books make me happiest. I love to play, write, and listen to music, and read good books with detail and suspense. These are my only ways to get away from people who are always telling me that I need to work harder.

Boy, 16, Georgia

I'm happiest at home with my dog. He doesn't want anything more of me than to rub his tummy, feed him, and give him lots of love.

Girl, 16, Pennsylvania

The thing that makes me happiest at home is when I have a chance to just relax and do something silly—or even babyish! When I can take an afternoon and read children's books, watch a video of a TV show I loved when I was little, color in a coloring book, or snuggle up with my favorite dolly and a nice, warm blanket, I am very content. I guess that's a little pathetic, but it makes me feel good inside because it's pressure-free, allowing me to just let go of all the responsibilities and worries that go along with being 17 years old.

Girl, 17, New Jersey

I am not happy at home. I feel uncomfortable being there. I have a job, so that gets me out of the house often. If I'm not working, I'll just go to a coffee shop and read, or to the library.

Boy, 17, Kansas

My sister makes me happiest at home. She doesn't really care how I do in school and so we can just relax and have fun. I don't ever have to worry about her looking at me in a different way.

Girl, 19, Oklahoma

There are so many ways to relax—listening to music, snuggling with your pet, keeping a diary, rock climbing, reading in a quiet corner of your room, chatting with friends online, and even "calculating vectors while watching **Fear Factor**," as one teen said in this section. When do you feel the most comfortable, relaxed, or refreshed at home? If you feel overscheduled or stressed, figure out something you can give up—or DEcrease—so you can INcrease your down time. You deserve it.

# Here Comes the Future

**W**hen gifted kids grow up they become . . . gifted adults. So what does *that* mean? Will the issues you face today due to your giftedness (such as boredom, perfectionism, and lack of intellectual peers) go away when you get older? Will they get worse? How will your gifts contribute to your future—your career, your relationships, and your imprint on the world? Are you optimistic? Hopeful? Nervous?

Will your career choice be one of the three so often chosen by gifted teens—doctor, lawyer, or engineer—or does your future lie elsewhere? Will you have a family? If you have kids, and they are gifted, what will you teach them about being gifted?

In short, what's in store for you?

That's a lot to think about. You won't know what the future holds until you get there, of course, but if you're like most gifted teens, you're eager to move into the next phase of your life. You're probably nervous too. After all, those expectations can weigh a lot (see chapter three)! Most everyone feels some fear and some hope. In this chapter, you can compare your own goals and dreams to those of other gifted young people.

## What would you like to learn that you haven't yet learned?

Right now, I'm working on novels written in verse.

Girl, 13, Ontario

Simply everything! I often wonder whether being immortal would solve the problem of having to choose a life specialization, but it is a useless wish. Instead, I'm going to learn as much as I can about everything from multiverse and string theory to animal and plant form and function. Also, prosthetics is amazing and a topic of interest, especially the mechanical and electrical engineering aspects of it. Biophysics, oceanography, and pi are also high on my list. There is simply not enough time!

Boy, 13, New York

Someday, I would like to go to another country overseas and explore a huge castle—maybe even sleep in one, especially if it is abandoned.

Girl, 14, Ohio

I want to learn French. I haven't had time to take French because I'm in band in middle school, and we only get one elective.

Girl, 14, Texas

I would like to learn more about the past, not necessarily U.S. history. We just read a book called *The Devil's Arithmetic,* which was about the Holocaust. I'd *really* like to learn more.

Boy, 14, Michigan

I am interested in the political and religious systems of other countries. Of course, we never talk about these in school.

Boy, 15, Indiana

I want to learn about pitching in baseball. It's all physics, trajectory and velocity, so I ought to be able to figure out how to do it well.

Boy, 15, Virginia

Law, because it leaves me in awe. Even though some people can't imagine a 4′ 10″ girl being an attorney, I can!

Girl, 16, Indiana

I am absolutely fascinated with autoimmune diseases. Particularly, I would like to find out why Raynaud's Phenomenon happens and find an effective way to treat it.

Girl, 16, Pennsylvania

I want to learn about outer space and the deepest depths of the ocean.

Boy, 17, Tennessee

I want to have hands-on experiences in hospital emergency rooms. Not just a biology course, but the real thing.

Boy, 17, Oklahoma

Eastern religions and philosophies, as well as advanced physics, are of most interest to me. It's not usually lack of time, but lack of people in those areas to talk to or learn from.

Boy, 17, Nebraska

"I want to learn about pitching in baseball. It's all physics, trajectory and velocity, so I ought to be able to figure out how to do it well."

## Reflection Connection

If you could choose any person, living or dead, which historical, literary, musical, athletic, or other individual would you like to share a dinner with? Why? What would you talk about?

## What are your future plans?

I hope to go to college at Ohio State University with an unknown major. Then, I hope to go to another four-year school to obtain my master's degree, followed by a job as a veterinarian. I want to live out my life helping animals.

Boy, 13, Ohio

To achieve. To know. To learn. To grow upwards. To explore the full range of my abilities. To write. To express. To discover. To impart. To teach. To communicate.

Girl, 13, England

I am going to become a grade school teacher, because I love to help little kids. I want to teach them basic stuff about school and life. I'll be a teacher my whole life until I retire when I am *really* old.

Girl, 13, Texas

I want to become a Federal Air Marshal and then earn my pilot's license.

Boy, 13, Ohio

Right now, I want to be a bone doctor or a journalist. It's funny that there is hardly any relation between the two, yet I still want to be both.

Boy, 14, Maryland

Well, I'm just going with the flow right now, so I'll figure it out in high school. I like doing makeup and hair, I like writing mysteries, and I love to cook. So . . . we'll see!

Girl, 14, Tennessee

I have plans to be a physical therapist or teacher, and one of my nonacademic goals is to go parasailing before I am 21.

Girl, 14, Louisiana

My future plans are to finish college and get a good job. I don't want to get pregnant until I am ready for a crying baby.

Girl, 14, Texas

I want to be a paperback writer. Maybe I'll write a book you'll want to read!

Boy, 14, Connecticut

I'm not sure what I want to major in yet, perhaps law or engineering, or aerospace technology. Or, perhaps, elementary education. After that I will live alone until I feel I have my life completely started. Then, I'll settle down and be an active part of a small community.

Girl, 15, Iowa

When I get to college, I want to study aeronautical engineering. During some point in my life, I want to be a professional tennis player. That's about it for right now, but I'm sure I'll add a lot more plans in the future.

Boy, 15, Arizona

Since I am very interested in eyes, I would like to study to be an optometrist. Who knows, though? Maybe my mind will change in a few years, so my backup plan right now is to become a lawyer.

Girl, 15, Colorado

I want to get married during college and then study to become a high school English teacher, and later a school administrator, before I retire.

Girl, 15, Indiana

I really have no idea what to become. Every time I consider a career, it is always shattered by the reality of the job and how much school the profession entails.

Boy, 16, Wisconsin

Since my family doesn't have much money, I will not be able to go to a college that is not near home. I have set my standards and goals extremely low, I'm afraid.

Girl, 16, Texas

I'd like to go to a really good school in hopes that there will be other gifted people like me there. If I don't go to college, I may work in construction, or perhaps take up a craft or trade. I'm really not sure. If all else fails, I would like to be a street poet in San Francisco.

Boy, 17, Kansas

After years of working as a psychiatrist, doctor, lawyer, or engineer, I want to be able to retire and enjoy my grandchildren and spoil them while traveling a whole lot with my loyal husband.

Girl, 17, Virginia

"Every time I consider a career, it is always shattered by the reality of the job and how much school the profession entails."

## Reflection Connection

Many gifted teens possess "multipotential," which is the interest in and ability to perform a number of careers with equal success. Although multipotential can be seen as an asset, it also can be a burden, because it's hard to know exactly what it is you'd like to spend your life doing—so many careers sound appealing! If you have multipotential, is it more of an asset or a burden for you? Why? What steps can you take now to explore several career options to help you make a more informed decision?

## Imagine you are 50 years old. Reflect back on your life's accomplishments.

As a 50-year-old, I'll probably reflect back on something I built as an engineer. I would have probably built something that revolutionized the automobile industry. I might also be reflecting on a time when I caught a huge fish. Of course, I don't know what the future holds for me, but I hope it is mostly good things.

Boy, 13, Texas

I headed up some of the biggest drug busts of all time. I have raised two wonderful children. I now have enough money to live happily in retirement.

Boy, 14, Maine

I hope by then that I have helped at least a thousand people and not charged them anything. I just want to look back and see that I have helped people better their lives. I just want to help.

Girl, 14, New Mexico

I had fun times, hard times, and sad times, but I stuck through it all the way.

Boy, 15, Iowa

I can't do that. I don't want to. There's so much I want to do—everything, in fact. I want my life to be a continual surprise.

Girl, 15, Illinois

After college graduation, I moved away, purchased a home with my husband, adopted a few children, and opened my own school for gifted children. At 60, I moved to Florida and became a golf junkie.

Girl, 15, Indiana

I'd like to think I was the all-time leader in strikeouts in the Mars Baseball League, did a lot of interesting and cool stuff in computer science and math, and maybe even had kids of my own. No, that's too weird. I can't imagine 50!

Boy, 16, Arkansas

I went to college as the young African-American woman that I am. I got over every obstacle that blocked my way, and I worked hard to become a successful doctor.

Girl, 16, Michigan

I'm not sure what I will have done, but I hope I will be proud of whatever I accomplished and the choices I made.

Boy, 17, Wisconsin

I have retired after twenty years of serving my country in the U.S. Air Force. I have a wife and three children, and I regularly explore the world, for its secrets are endless.

Boy, 18, Tennessee

I might die before I am 50. This makes me want to cry.

Boy, 18, Alabama

Do you think issues like boredom, perfectionism, and high expectations will go away or become easier to deal with as you get older? Of all the obstacles you face now due to your giftedness, which ones do you think will linger on beyond the school years, and which ones are likely to be resolved (or reduced) upon high school or college graduation? Why?

## Are you hopeful?

With new technologies, despite the chaos it might bring, the world will be a better place in the future because of a few strong individuals. Physically, emotionally, or intellectually, these people will grasp onto ideas to better the world. I hope I can be one of those people.

Girl, 13, New Jersey

I am not hopeful because we are still all going to die. Yes, I dream and wish for some things, but overall, cynicism is safer.

Girl, 13, Ontario

It depends on what you mean by this question. If you mean *my* future then, yes, I am very hopeful. If you are talking about the *world's* future, then my answer is no.

Boy, 14, Connecticut

"I do feel hopeful about the future because I have a lot of support in my life. I believe in myself and others believe in me."

I do feel hopeful about the future because I have a lot of support in my life. Also, I always do everything to the best of my ability and I think that quality is going to help me. My parents support me a lot and that motivates me to have positive ways of thinking about my life. I have hope because I believe in myself and others believe in me.

Girl, 14, California

I always say, "When bad comes, there is always good behind it," because you can't go through life dwelling on the negative. You'd be miserable.

Girl, 14, Ohio

I don't think life will get better *or* worse. Every day is the same for me.

Boy, 14, Massachusetts

Every door I come to is open and while that is a little scary, I know I'll make the right decisions when I need to.

Girl, 15, Iowa

I have this theory that if you think of the worst, that's how things are going to work out, so I always think of the best.

Boy, 15, Illinois

Am I hopeful? So much so that I believe the Cubs will win the World Series next year, or maybe the year after that.

Boy, 15, North Carolina

My friends make me feel hopeful because they're good people with the same high standards I have. With God, my parents, and my friends, there is nothing not to be hopeful about.

Boy, 15, Texas

The future is what I live for—I can't wait! I know it is going to be great!

Girl, 16, Indiana

143

I can't really say that I feel hopeful about the future in general. I find myself quite disgusted with the way society is today, and I think that can only worsen over time. Overall, people are ill-mannered, uneducated, and overly dependent on technology. All people seem to care about is careers, dieting, and being sexy. I often wonder if people remember how to THINK. If I could, I'd start my own world from scratch. Most days I think that the one we're on now is messed up beyond repair.

Girl, 17, New Jersey

Being secure in my abilities and potential, I know I will succeed.

Boy, 17, Tennessee

Living in a small town in the rural Midwest has really drained a lot of hope out of me. I doubt that I'll marry, and I'm not sure I'll be motivated enough to make it through college.

Boy, 18, Nebraska

# In Their Words: Elizabeth, Age 21

My name is Elizabeth and I am a recovering underachiever. I was born and raised in the suburbs of Houston. My mother was an elementary school teacher and my father worked for NASA. As a child, I would occasionally find myself in the midst of one of my parents' adult events—a quick trip to the office with my dad, or a luncheon with my mom's friends. Inevitably, an adult we ran into at these events would ask the question (posed by all well-intentioned adults who liked to consider themselves "good with children"): "What do you want to be when you grow up?" I never gave a standard answer; instead, I would say that I hoped to become a chemist or a teacher, perhaps an astronaut or a doctor or a spy, or, if I wanted to give my parents a bit of a jolt, a freelance artist. But the real answer, the secret answer that I never shared with anyone, was this: I wanted to be great!

⟶

Heracles, Julius Caesar, Leonardo da Vinci, Queen Elizabeth I, Madame Curie, Neil Armstrong, Georgia O'Keeffe—they haunted me from an early age. "Human beings can do incredible things!" my childhood ghosts would cry out from the storybook illustrations I held in my lap. If only I could wait patiently, make it through my teen years, I, too, would be able to shape the world in extraordinary ways.

Fast forward about a decade. I'm standing in the middle of a parking lot momentarily blinded by the Texas sun. A hideous, cheap plastic graduation robe is tossed over my shoulder. In my sticky arms, I'm grasping a stack full of certificates acknowledging my tenure as class president and involvement in virtually all of our school's extracurricular activities. Clenched between my lips I have a few ribbons for academic merit. And in the pit of my stomach, I have a deep sense of unaccomplishment. Despite the armful of awards that seem to shout "model student," I know the truth—I had never written a paper any earlier than the night before it was due, and "studying" for me consisted of cracking open the textbook for only the second or third time in that semester. The glowing sense of victory I had always expected to show up at high school graduation had stood me up.

"But honestly," I say to myself as I stuff my robe, papers, medals, and diploma unceremoniously into the trunk of my car, "what else could I have done? It's not *my* fault that everything was always so easy." And as I zoom forward on the freeway, my mind floats backwards lazily to those first awkward years of high school.

One social studies teacher walked into the room, clapping his hands brusquely. "Okay, class, we have three weeks until the end of the school year and ten chapters to cover. Turn to the section on the Korean War."

We opened our books.

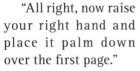
"All right, now raise your right hand and place it palm down over the first page."

We looked around at each other, confused, but followed his instructions. "Now, we've *covered* it," said the teacher, his chins jiggling as he chuckled at the pun. "Let's move on."

"We're not going to learn about the Korean War?" protested one student.

"You don't need to know about the Korean War unless you're Korean."

A hand shot up in the back of the room. "I'm Korean."

"Oh . . . well, you can read the chapter on your own."

Unfortunately, this was the norm rather than the exception for a great chunk of my time in school.

Almost a year after my depressingly anticlimactic high school graduation, I'm sitting at an enormous round table in an honors history seminar, delivering a presentation on the Korean War's implications for the Vietnam War—which I put a grueling half-hour into preparing. "As I'm sure you know," I say, looking up nervously from my notes, "Korea is quite close to China, so it's no surprise that the Chinese leadership was interested in preventing an American presence in the regions of Korea closest to their country."

"You mean the part of Korea that *borders* China?" asks a student.

(Korea borders China? That was certainly news to me!)

"Heh, heh. Yes, that's exactly what I meant: the part of Korea that *borders* China." The entire class stares back at me as though they suspect I've never seen a map of Asia. I feel tiny pin pricks on my face as the blood rushes to my cheeks.

Half an hour later, as I'm packing my books, papers, pens, and shame into my bag, it occurs to me that despite the acute probability

→

that my high school history teacher was perhaps negligent in his instruction, *he* was not the one turning bright pink from embarrassment at this moment.

So while I did go home and pull up a map of the eastern hemisphere online, the big lesson I learned was that being "great" is about more than attaining that perfect GPA, or getting into your dream college, or building a resume that takes half a ream of paper to print. It's about tackling every challenge head on—giving it your all, so to speak. Along the way, people may give you papers stating that you are wonderful, or small glass sculptures with your name on the bottom, or even money to go to college. These will all be nice, but they are not the point of all your efforts. I'm sure Shakespeare never said to himself, "Oh, one hit play is good enough for me. The public already adores me. I think I'll retire now."

> "Despite the acute possibility that my high school history teacher was perhaps negligent in his instruction, HE was not the one turning bright pink from embarrassment at this moment."

The point of approaching South Asian geography with a passionate ferocity, or reading the unabridged version of a book, or taking differential equations when pre-calculus would fulfill your math requirement, is so that when you run up against something that genuinely stumps you, you know that it's not because you've piddled away your time playing video games. The heroes of my childhood did not achieve immortality by measuring themselves against society's standards and expectations; they did it by exceeding their own. That is my constant struggle today. Sometimes I fall short (as evidenced by my recent French composition) but when I do tackle a challenge with the full force of my potential, it's as though the world is mine to grasp. I feel GREAT!

## Is there anything else you would like to share that we haven't asked about?

I wish you would have asked how others found more gifted kids like themselves. Even with most of my good friends, it's hard to relate to them.

Boy, 13, Massachusetts

You could have asked us about how realistic our dreams are. We all want our life dreams to come true, and we tell ourselves that we are going to try our hardest to attain them. But the truth is, most of us don't reach our highest dreams, and we settle for something lower. But I don't want to "settle." Once I pick a career, I'm going to try and try until I accomplish what I want.

Girl, 15, Ohio

I think you should have asked if we were on any medications. I developed sudden-onset OCD (Obsessive Compulsive Disorder) when I was 7 and have had to take medication ever since. I think kids who are really smart and don't have a neurological problem are really lucky. The OCD is one of the reasons I rely on my parents so much; I couldn't make it without them.

Boy, 15, North Carolina

You needed to ask about loneliness and depression. Ask us whether we find our parents to be immature. Ask us about how we pursue our passions at home. Ask whether we have anyone to talk to about these passions and where we found our passions in the first place. Ask whether our siblings are gifted, and how we feel about them. There's a lot more you could have asked.

Boy, 17, Kansas

I'm not sure what the question is, but the answer is "humor." Humor is incredibly important; it's how you get through each day. Some things are so bad that if you can't find some way to laugh yourself through them, they will drag you down forever.

Boy, 17, Virginia

# Keep It Going

**W**hen we first thought about asking teens to share their views on growing up gifted, we knew we would receive intelligent and interesting anecdotes. What surprised us was just how many gifted teens wanted to share their views with us. Thousands of responses arrived, each one adding a piece to the puzzle of what it means to be a gifted adolescent.

The voice of each contributor is unique, compelling, and valuable on its own, yet taken together these teens' words teach us something larger: that some peers, some friends, some schools, and some families are amazingly supportive of gifted kids—while others, sadly, are not. We hope that, whether your own environment is super-supportive or otherwise, you'll take strength from this book and the knowledge that you're part of a very real community. If *More Than a Test Score* sends one strong and focused message it is that you and other gifted teens are not alone. We hope the honesty shared in these pages will resonate for years to come in the minds and hearts of readers seeking information and solace, comfort and connection.

And we have one more hope: that this book is the beginning of an ongoing dialogue about giftedness you have with other gifted kids, teens, and adults. The voices shared in this book will reach thousands of adolescents, educators, and parents who need to hear them—but you, too, must carry the message personally to those in your life who matter to you. You have the right to an appropriate education, to be understood as the intelligent individual you are, and to have your hopes and dreams taken seriously by others. By being willing to talk, you can encourage and support other gifted people, as well. Change and improvement for gifted teens will happen one person at a time—starting with you.

Enjoy the ride, and feel free to enter the conversation by contacting us (and others) with your thoughts and opinions. Those who care will listen.

# About the Authors

 Robert A. Schultz, Ph.D., spends the majority of his life helping raise his children. He spends "spare" time as an associate professor of gifted education and curriculum studies at the University of Toledo (Ohio). A man of many hats, Bob coordinates the university's Middle Grades Teacher Education program; travels the country as a consultant in Gifted Education and Curriculum Development/Evaluation; teaches in public schools; researches and writes about giftedness; and, most importantly to his kids, is a hockey coach.

Bob and his wife, Cindy, live in Toledo, Ohio, but eventually they will retire and while away their time sailing in the Caribbean. Until then, Bob plans to continue helping parents, kids, teachers, and schools meet the diverse needs of gifted learners in and out of classrooms.

 James R. Delisle, Ph.D., is distinguished professor of education at Kent State University in Ohio, where he directs the undergraduate and graduate programs in gifted child education. He is a former classroom teacher, special education teacher, and teacher of gifted children (and still teaches gifted seventh- and eighth-graders one day a week). He has received several teaching honors, including Kent State University's most prestigious distinction, the Distinguished Teaching Award, in 2004. However, the most important award came recently when one of his former fourth-grade students selected him, upon high school graduation, as his "Most Inspirational Teacher." Jim also has served as a counselor for gifted adolescents and their families. He is the author or coauthor of more than 200 articles and 14 books, including the best-selling *Gifted Kids' Survival Guide: A Teen Handbook* and *When Gifted Kids Don't Have All the Answers: How to Meet Their Social and Emotional Needs* (both with Judy Galbraith).

Jim and his wife, Deb, live in Kent, Ohio, most of the year and in North Myrtle Beach, South Carolina, when school is out.

Bob and Jim also are the coauthors of *Smart Talk: What Kids Say About Growing Up Gifted.*

# Other Great Books from Free Spirit

### Smart Talk
What Kids Say About Growing Up Gifted
*by Robert A. Schultz, Ph.D., and James R. Delisle, Ph.D.*
Quotes from real kids ages 6–12 and brief biographies
provide insight into challenges gifted children face, like
trying to fit in, dealing with adults' expectations, making
mistakes, and being bored in school. Activities help readers
relate the information and issues to their own lives.
For ages 12 & under.
*$13.95; 128 pp.; softcover; illust.; 6" x 9"*

### Perfectionism
What's Bad About Being Too Good?
Revised and Updated Edition
*by Miriam Adderholdt, Ph.D., and Jan Goldberg*
This revised and updated edition includes new research
and statistics on the causes and consequences of perfectionism, biographical sketches of famous perfectionists and risk
takers, and resources for readers who want to know more.
For ages 13 & up.
*$12.95; 136 pp.; softcover; illust.; 6" x 9"*

### The Gifted Kids' Survival Guide
A Teen Handbook
Revised, Expanded, and Updated Edition
*by Judy Galbraith, M.A., and Jim Delisle, Ph.D.*
Vital information on giftedness, IQ, school success, col-
lege planning, stress, perfectionism, and much more.
For ages 11–18.
*$15.95; 304 pp.; softcover; illust.; 7¹/₄" x 9¹/₄"*

## Fast, Friendly, and Easy to Use
# www.freespirit.com

**Browse the catalog**

**Info & extras**

**Many ways to search**

**Quick check-out**

**Stop in and see!**

**1.800.735.7323 • fax 612.337.5050 • help4kids@freespirit.com**